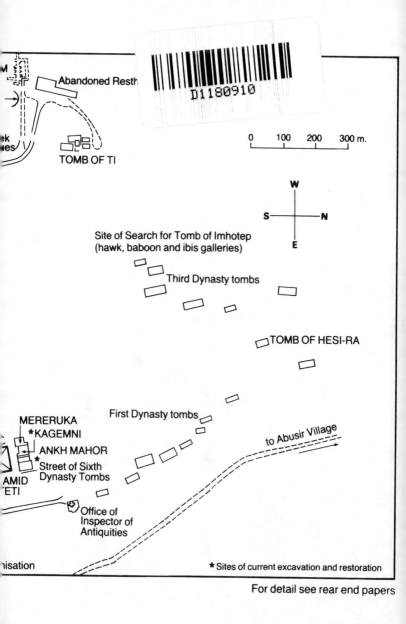

Abandoned Resth...

TOMB OF TI

0 100 200 300 m.

W

S ——┼—— N

E

Site of Search for Tomb of Imhotep
(hawk, baboon and ibis galleries)

Third Dynasty tombs

TOMB OF HESI-RA

First Dynasty tombs

to Abusir Village

MERERUKA
*KAGEMNI
ANKH MAHOR
*
Street of Sixth
Dynasty Tombs

AMID
ETI

Office of
Inspector of
Antiquities

nisation

* Sites of current excavation and restoration

For detail see rear end papers

SAKKARA
and MEMPHIS

A Guide to the Necropolis
and the Ancient Capital

Second Edition

Jill Kamil

Original photographs by Ann Stuart Anderson
Research for maps and diagrams by Elizabeth Rodenbeck

LONGMAN
LONDON AND NEW YORK

Longman Group Limited
Longman House, Burnt Mill, Harlow,
Essex CM20 2JE, England
and Associated companies throughout the world

Longman Inc.,
1560 Broadway,
New York, NY 10036

© Longman Group Ltd 1978 and 1985

Photographs © Ann Stuart Anderson, except for pages 47, 61, 98 and 117 (Lehnert and Landrock, Cairo) and page 71 (the Committee of the Egypt Exploration Society).

First published 1978
Second edition 1985

British Library Cataloguing in Publication Data

Kamil, Jill
Sakkara and Memphis: a guide to the necropolis
and ancient capital. — 2nd ed.
1. Necropolis of Memphis   2. Sakkara — Tombs
I. Title   II. Kamil, Jill. Sakkara: a guide
to the necropolis and the site of Memphis
916.2'2   DT73.S3

ISBN 0-582-78380-1

Library of Congress Cataloging in Publication Data

Kamil, Jill
Sakkara and Memphis.
Rev. ed. of: Sakkara.   London; New York : Longman, 1978.
Bibliography: p.185
Includes index.
1. Ṣaqqārah (Egypt) — Antiquities — Guide-books.
2. Memphis (Ancient city) — Guide-books.
3. Egypt — Antiquities — Guide-books.   I. Kamil, Jill. Sakkara.
II. Title.
DT73.S3K35   1984   932   84-28898
ISBN 0-582-78380-1

The author would like to thank the late Labib Habachi, Egypt's most distinguished Egyptologist, formerly Director of Field Work of the Antiquities Department and Member of the Institut d'Egypte, for his advice, help and encouragement in up-dating this Second Edition.

Produced by Longman Group (FE) Ltd
Printed in Hong Kong

Dedicated to Timmy and Ricky
with love

CONTENTS

Page

*Well-known monuments.

MAPS AND DIAGRAMS

PREFACE

Sakkara is one of the richest archaeological sites in Egypt, containing monuments constructed over a span of more than three thousand years. The earliest were mastabas of the pharaohs of the 1st Dynasty, and the latest structures date to Graeco-Roman and even to Christian times.

Any attempt to conform to the practice of writing a guidebook to the area in order of the historical importance of the monuments, their state of preservation, or convenience to tourists, would defeat the purpose of the book, which is to place the monuments in their historical and cultural perspective so that Egypt's complex ancient history may be more easily understood by the layman.

The monuments of Sakkara have therefore been grouped in chronological order. The Introduction, which briefly outlines the history of Memphis, provides the framework and also serves as cross reference for Chapter 7 on Memphis. The Table of Kings confines itself to the pharaohs of the first six dynasties, since Sakkara is primarily an Old Kingdom burial ground, and it was the period in which Memphis rose to be the capital of Egypt.

In this Second Edition the following additions have been made: Chapter 6 has been enlarged to include the recent discovery of New Kingdom tombs on the necropolis; Chapter 7 has been re-written in the light of renewed archaeological interest in Memphis; Chapter 8 has been updated to include Work in Progress during the 1983/4 archaeological season. Also, three new maps have been provided: the two rear end maps are enlargements of the areas lying to the south of the Step Pyramid Complex, and to the north of the Pyramid of Teti. A map of Memphis appears on page 158.

10

MAP OF THE NILE VALLEY

CHAPTER 1   INTRODUCTION

Egypt has an unbroken story of human progress longer than can be traced anywhere else on earth. Its ancient civilisation dominated the eastern Mediterranean at a time when Europe, America and most of western Asia were still in the Stone Age, and only came to an end with the conquest of Alexander the Great in 332 B.C. One of the main causes of the remarkable homogeneity and continuity of the ancient civilisation lies in the special physical characteristics of the country.

Egypt is a land of unusual geographic isolation, with well-defined boundaries. To the north is the Mediterranean. To the east are the Arabian desert and the Red Sea. The limitless expanses of the Sahara desert stretch to the west. And to the south, beyond Aswan, lie the Cataracts, successive rapids where the rocky formations infringe on the river, and the arid desert packs close against the hills to east and west of the confined valley. Flowing between Egypt's southern and northern borders is the Nile, one of many rivers to rise in equatorial Africa, but the only one to traverse northern Africa. It travels over 4,000 miles and finds an outlet in the Mediterranean Sea. Before the construction of the High Dam the monsoon rains on the Ethiopian highlands caused the waters of the Blue Nile to swell and bear silt-laden waters to Egypt each year. When the flood withdrew, a layer of rich, black and extremely fertile soil had been deposited on the banks of the river and in the Delta.

The division of Egypt into the 'Two Lands', Upper and Lower Egypt, is both physical and climatic. Upper Egypt lies south of the apex of the Delta and is mostly barren, apart from the narrow ribbon of verdant land flanking the river, which represents the limits to which the waters of the Nile reach during flood; the average summer temperature is 50°C, the average winter temperature is 20°C, and the air, especially in the south, is extremely dry. Lower Egypt, the triangle of the Delta, is completely fertile and the climate is temperate; temperatures range from an average of

30°C in summer to 13°C in winter.

The earliest inhabitants of the Nile valley were hunters, who tracked game across the grasslands that once covered northern Africa from the eastern Sudan to Algeria, as well as nomadic tribes of Asiatic origin who filtered into Egypt in sporadic migrations across the Sinai Peninsula and the Red Sea. Late Paleolithic settlements (c. 12000 to 8000 B.C.) reveal that these people, as well as the indigenous inhabitants, at first remained isolated from one another. Flaked tools alongside animal and fish remains on the shores of lakes and ancient streams indicate that totally divergent cultures evolved. These were destined to fuse, as the climatic conditions changed.

For gradually the weather became drier. Over several thousands of years there was decreasing rainfall. The waning of the waters of rivers and lakes, and the increased heat and evaporation caused the plants of the savanna to dry up and turn to dust. Meanwhile the river Nile, flowing more sluggishly, deposited additional silt along its banks and in the Delta, the level of which rose higher each year. The desolate wastes were known from early times as the Red Land. The Black Land, which gave its name to the country as *Kemt*, was the life-giving land of Egypt. It was a sharply defined world of life and death.

Though the country's natural boundaries were deterrents against would-be invaders, they were by no means barriers providing serious obstacles against outside influences. Tribes from Asia, Libya and southern Africa continued to cross the intervening areas and make their way towards Egypt. As they drew away from the scorching desert towards the river, their lives became slowly, unavoidably, bound to the ebb and flow of the annual flood. That is to say, as the water rose each year in July they were obliged to draw back from the banks. By August, when the river waters swept unharnessed across the lowlands, turning Egypt into a vast lake, they took to the highland plateau and pursued hunting activities, tracking antelope, hartebeest, wild ass and gazelle with lances, bows and arrows. During the first half of October the river attained its highest level and thereafter began to subside, leaving lagoons and streams which afforded natural reservoirs for fish. A variety of plants grew from the fertile, uniform deposit of silt, providing ideal conditions for food-collecting. During this season of plenty, hunting was at a minimum. From January to March seasonal pools dried out, fishing was limited, but in the swampy areas near the river there were turtles, rodents and Nile clams. At low Nile, during

April, May and June, game scattered, food became scarce, and hunting was actively pursued once more. Despite their diverse origins, therefore, there was a natural tendency for the people to group together during the 'season of abundance' and to split up into smaller groups during the low-flood season or during periods of drought.

As a certain rhythm formed in their lives, they observed that the gifts of their naturally irrigated valley depended on a dual force; the sun and the river, both of which had creative power and destructive power. For the sun that cast its benevolent rays on the land also created the desiccated wastes of the desert, and the Nile that brought its turbid waters to revitalise the soil could sweep destructively across the valley. These two phenomena, moreover, shared in the pattern of death and rebirth and made a profound impression on the people: the sun that sailed across the heavens and 'died' on the western horizon each evening was 'reborn' in the eastern sky the following morning; and the river was directly and unfailingly responsible for the 'rebirth' of the crop after the 'death' of the land each year. This natural sequence of rebirth

Fishing from papyrus skiffs. (Tomb of Kagemni)

14

after death undoubtedly lay at the root of the ancient Egyptian conviction in the afterlife. As inevitably as the sun rose each morning and the flood arrived each year, man, it was believed, would rise and live again. Rebirth was a deeply rooted concept because it arose from awareness of nature's changeless cycles.

The earliest evidence we have that the ancient Egyptians believed in the afterlife comes from the burial customs of an Upper Egyptian settlement called Badari (*c.* 4000 B.C.). This burial ground is situated at the edge of the desert. The graves were simple oval pits into which the deceased, wrapped in matting or skins, was placed. Surrounding the body were his worldly possessions: weapons, bone needles and awls, hunting gear, ointments and various pieces of jewellery, which suggest that they may have been considered necessary to ensure an afterlife similar to the earthly experience. In addition there was dark grey pottery containing food and drink, which would evince a belief that sustenance was required for the survival of some aspect of the deceased which did not perish with the body. We know from the religious customs of later times that one of the immortal aspects of man was known as the *Ka* or 'double'. This was a sort of guardian spirit, shown as two uplifted arms, believed to be born with man, to live with him throughout his life and, if properly nourished and provided for, to continue to live after the *Khat*, 'the body' or outer shell, had perished. It was to overcome the risk of exposure of the body to the elements and thereby destroying the repository for the *Ka*, that a mound of rubble or brick was placed over the grave pit. As progressively more care was devoted to improving and strengthening this mound, it was eventually formed into a durable rectangular superstructure with sloping walls over the tomb chamber, which has become known as the *mastaba* (Arabic word for 'bench'). The *Ka* was believed to dwell in the mummy and inside the tomb, but could also abide outside of it. Thus the necropolis was a city of *Kas*.

Another immortal aspect of man was the *Ba*, or 'soul', shown as a bird with the head of the deceased, which came into existence only after the death of the individual. The *Ba* was believed to escape the confines of the body and soar to heaven on the broad rays of the sun. It was for the projection of the *Ba* to heaven that the priests performed rituals and prayers in Mortuary Temples. Once these were accomplished, the deceased became a divine or supernatural power known as the *Akh*. The shining stars in the heavens were believed to be the *Akhw* of the deceased. While the *Ka* belonged to the earth, the *Ba* and *Akhw* belonged to the heavens.

Other important elements of man were his *Ib*, his heart, considered the centre of conscious thought and a guide to his conscience, and his *Ren*, his name, which was necessary for identification.

It is believed that agriculture was introduced into the Nile valley about 5000 B.C. The cultivation and storage of grain (a variety of domesticated barley brought from Asia) resulted in a slow movement away from hunting and fishing as an economic activity. Once grain could be stored and people were assured of a regular food supply, they could settle down. And since it was not necessary for all the community to devote their efforts to farming, some members began to specialise in the production of improved weapons, tools and implements. Flint-making was mastered, stone vessels were fashioned, palettes or slates for grinding cosmetics were carved in the form of birds, animals and fish, the artistic quality of which indicates that the people were no longer primarily concerned with survival.

The Ka *of the deceased was an immortal aspect that could inhabit the statue. (Copy of a statue of Zoser).*

The various settlements at first remained self-contained, but slowly a process of assimilation took place. Some villages may have coalesced as their boundaries expanded, or small groups of people possibly gravitated towards larger ones and started to trade and barter with them. As they became more dependent on one another, there was a natural fusion into larger social units, which are the origin of the various nomes or 'provinces' of Upper and Lower Egypt which formed the basis of the political structure of Egypt in historic times.

Gradually the affairs of the various villages became tied to a major settlement, which undoubtedly represented the richest and most powerful of them. This tendency towards political unity occurred in both Upper and Lower Egypt. In Upper Egypt the chief settlement, or capital, was Nekhen, where the leader, the pharaoh, wore a conical White Crown and took the sedge plant as his emblem. In the Delta the capital was Buto, and the pharaoh wore the characteristic Red Crown and adopted the bee as his symbol.

Decorations on pre-dynastic pottery show that the different communities of Upper and Lower Egypt identified themselves with emblems or totems on standards. There were standards bearing the emblems of the Upper Egyptian capital of Nekhen (the vulture) and the Delta capital of Buto (the cobra). There were also standards bearing emblems of two crossed arrows and a shield, which became the symbols of the huntress-goddess Neith of Sais in the Delta; two fossils, which was the symbol of Min the fertility god of Coptos in Upper Egypt; and emblems of Anubis the jackal, Selket the scorpion, and Hathor the cow. There were also emblems of Horus and Set, who feature prominently in ancient Egyptian mythology; Horus, the hawk, was the traditional totem of settlers in the fertile Delta, and Set, a hybrid animal with pointed ears and nose perhaps representing an anteater, was associated with the arid desert of Upper Egypt. The emblem of a settlement was undoubtedly carried into battle for identification, and a leader became identified with the emblem that brought him luck. When the clan of the Horus hawk at one time triumphed over their enemies, the victorious leader proudly prefixed his name with that of the hawk, which thenceforth became the symbol of strength and power, and, ultimately, of royalty.

The term 'god' or 'goddess' in this context is, of course, misleading. For there is no indication that the people actually worshipped the emblems that distinguished their different localities.

A frieze of cobra, emblem of Buto in the Delta. (Zoser's Complex – southwest corner of Great Court)

Later, in historic times, when provinces rose to power, local deities were promoted politically and accredited with diverse powers. But in prehistoric times, all that we can say for certain is that groups of settlers chose ensigns from the natural phenomena of their districts or from birds, animals or water creatures common to the area; and that the rhythm of their lives, which affected their cultures, their religious beliefs and, ultimately, their political development, was based both on the inevitability of life after death as demonstrated by the sun and the river, and on a natural 'dualism' in Egypt: the arid desert and the fertile soil; Upper Egypt and Lower Egypt.

Despite the tendency towards regionalisation, Egypt lacked the necessary compactness for political unity. With a straggling 1,200-kilometre-long barren area to the south, and a sprawling fertile Delta in the north, cultural differences persisted long after the so-called 'unification' by King Menes, the pharaoh who stands at the beginning of recorded history. In fact the only two factors that neutralised the differences between the Two Lands were the vital artery that flowed between them, and the ever-present sunshine. It is not surprising, therefore, that two of the earliest religious cults were solar and nature. The solar cult featured Ra, the Sun-god, in the role of the creation, and concerned his daily cycle across the sky. The nature cult featured Osiris.

The Osiris myth, which is probably rooted in legend, underwent modification and embellishment from generation to generation, and variation from province to province. Osiris is believed to have once been a chieftain in Busiris, one of the provinces of the Delta, and after his death was so venerated by his people that he became associated in their minds with a harvest deity of the area. He became a deity associated with water and with the death and rebirth of the land. The most well-known version of the myth is that of Plutarch A.D. 46–120. It is, however, an end product, a combination of all the variations on the theme devised by the Greek writers from fragmentary allusions and oral tradition, and is full of contradictions. However, according to this version, Osiris was a just and much loved ruler who taught his people the arts of making agricultural implements, rotating crops and controlling the waters of the Nile. He also taught them how to adapt to a corn diet, and to produce bread, wine and beer.

Osiris had a wife, Isis, who was equally loved and who taught the people how to grind corn and to weave linen with a loom; and with her devotion to her husband, Isis intimated the benefits of domestic life. Osiris also had a brother, Set, who was jealous of his popularity and secretly aspired to his position of favour. Having taken the measurements of his brother's body, Set had a handsome coffer constructed, and at a feast, when all the guests were drinking and merrymaking, Set joked that he would give the coffer to whomsoever it fitted exactly. One after another the guests lay in the coffer, but it fitted none of them. Finally Osiris followed suit, at which point one of Set's accomplices ran and flung down the lid, hastily soldering it in position with molten lead. Then he flung the coffer into the Nile. (There are no traces of this version in ancient Egyptian texts, where the oldest sources indicate that Osiris was either assassinated or drowned in the 'new water', which was the annual flood.)

When Isis heard of the tragic news of her husband's disappearance, she put on the attire of mourning and travelled up and down the Nile seeking his body. She eventually found it and, with her sister Nephthys, prayed and crooned yearning incantations which restored breath to Osiris' body, movement to his limbs, and sight to his eyes; his seed entered Isis and she conceived Horus.

In another version, Isis hid the body, but Set was out boar-hunting and discovered the body. He forthwith tore it into fourteen pieces, which he scattered all over the land. Isis and Nephthys once again set out on their sorrowful mission. They collected the pieces and, according to one version, bound them together with bandages. According to another version they buried each piece where it was found. And yet a third version has it that only an image of Osiris was buried in each city, in order that Osiris might be worshipped in many places but that Set would never know the real grave. The head is believed to have been found in Abydos, which became the centre of the Osiris cult, and a holy city to which annual pilgrimage was made.

An Egyptian version of the myth describes the two sisters, Isis and Nephthys, lamenting over the body. Ra, the Sun-god, hears them and sends the jackal-headed Anubis, the ibis-headed Thoth, and the hawk-headed Horus to piece together the broken body of the murdered god and to swathe it in linen. Isis and Nephthys then fan the dead body with their wings in order to bring life back to him. Since, however, the resurrected Osiris could no longer rule on earth, his throne having been taken over by his son Horus, he thenceforth reigned as King of the Underworld.

In the resurrection of Osiris, the ancient Egyptians saw the pledge of eternity for themselves. They believed that all men could live eternally like Osiris, provided their friends and relatives would do for their body what the gods had done for that of Osiris.

Isis raised her son Horus in the marshes of the Delta until he was strong enough to set out in search of his father's murderer. The many and terrible battles between Horus and Set, which dominate ancient Egyptian mythology, were therefore battles between good and evil, as well as between the son of the pastoral god and the god of the desert. Horus, as already mentioned, was the traditional deity of Lower Egypt, which is largely fertile, and Set of Upper Egypt, which is almost barren.

The rivalry between Upper and Lower Egypt, if it existed in prehistory, arose from the geographical structure of the land. And the reason for the southerners from Nekhen (Hierakonpolis) pushing northwards from their confined valley towards the Delta was undoubtedly economic. It was probably a slow movement, that may have taken two or three generations to accomplish, though tradition accredits the legendary King Menes with a single victorious conquest.

Ancient Egyptian history was divided into thirty dynasties, from Menes to Alexander the Great, by an Egyptian priest called Manetho, in the reign of Ptolemy II, 285 to 247 B.C. The dynasties do not always follow genealogical order; they sometimes present a politico-religious change. However, the thirty dynasties have been grouped into three 'Great Periods' which are clearly defined: the Old Kingdom (3rd–6th Dynasties), the Middle Kingdom (11th–12th Dynasties) and the New Kingdom (18th–20th Dynasties). Between the Old and Middle Kingdoms was a period of political and social confusion and the rise of the provincial powers (known as the First Intermediate Period). Between the Middle and New Kingdoms was a period of foreign conquest by the Hyksos, who introduced the horse and chariot to Egypt (known as the Second Intermediate Period). After the fall of the New Kingdom was a period of decline, known as the Late Period, when foreign rulers took over the throne (21st–25th Dynasties), followed by a revival known as the Saite Period (26th Dynasty). Then came a period of national rule broken by the Persian conquests (27th–30th Dynasties), which came to an end with the Greek conquest in 332 B.C.

The Greek occupation, known as the Ptolemaic Period, lasted for about three centuries, until the Roman conquest in 30 B.C. Under the Emperor Theodosius (380 A.D.) Christianity became the state religion of Egypt. The Egyptian Christians are known as Copts. The Christian era, or Byzantine Period, lasted until the Arab conquest in 640 A.D.

The history of Memphis can be traced from its traditional foundation by Narmer (Menes) to its last official role as venue for discussions between the Arab conquerors and the leader of the Copts, a word derived from the Greek *Aigyptos*: Egypt.

Pharaonic period

	Dynasties	Dates
Early Dynastic Period	1st and 2nd	3100–2686 B.C.
OLD KINGDOM	3rd to 6th	2686–2181 B.C.
1st Intermediate Period	7th to early 11th	2181–2133 B.C.
MIDDLE KINGDOM	11th and 12th	2133–1786 B.C.
2nd Intermediate Period	13th to 17th	1786–1567 B.C.
NEW KINGDOM	18th to 20th	1567–1080 B.C.
Period of Decline	21st to 25th	1080–656 B.C.
Saite Period	26th	656–525 B.C.
Persian Period	27th to 30th	525–332 B.C.

Graeco-Roman Period

Ptolemaic Period	332–30 B.C.
Roman Period	30 B.C.–395 A.D.
Byzantine Period	395 A.D.–640 A.D.

Islamic Period

After the Islamic conquest in 640, Memphis was visited by what might be called the pre-Napoleonic Egyptologists. After Napoleon's expedition to Egypt in 1798, the era of scientific Egyptology began.

HISTORICAL FRAMEWORK

3100 B.C. EARLY DYNASTIC PERIOD
(1st and 2nd Dynasties)

Memphis was the chosen headquarters of Narmer (Menes), who united Upper and Lower Egypt and founded the 1st Dynasty. It was known as the 'White Wall' (a name it retained till Graeco-Roman times) and was strategically situated near the border between the Two Lands. At first it was probably no more than a simple fortification.

22

Relief of Ptah, God of Memphis.

In the 1st Dynasty, great monuments were constructed at Thinis near Abydos in Upper Egypt, the birthplace of the kings, and on the Sakkara plateau. It was at one time thought that the former was a cenotaph where relatives and friends could provide offerings, and that the actual tomb was at Sakkara. A more recent explanation (by no means confirmed) is that the kings were actually buried near Abydos, and that the massive tombs on the Sakkara plateau belonged to Viziers whose task it was to control the strategic fortification on the border between the Two Lands.

During the first two hundred years after the so-called unification, there was grave political unrest in the country. Successive pharaohs, who all bore a traditional Horus title, tried to consolidate the union by combining the different traditions of Upper and Lower Egypt in an attempt to create a single common culture; the White Crown of Upper Egypt and the Red Crown of Lower Egypt were combined into a 'Double Crown'. The cobra emblem, Edjo, of Buto (Pe) in Lower Egypt and the vulture emblem, Nekhbit, of Nekheb (El Kab) in Upper Egypt were combined into a 'Two Ladies', or *nebty*, title. And the sedge plant and the bee, emblems adopted by the leaders of Upper and Lower Egypt, were also combined into what is known as the *ni-sw-bity* title, which preceded their praenomen or enthronement name. Periods of harmony were, however, short-lived, and even a political marriage between an Upper Egyptian pharaoh and a Delta princess did not permanently put an end to the unrest. The natural antipathy between the settlers of Upper and of Lower Egypt undoubtedly rose from their cultural differences, which were the outcome of the physical characteristics of the Two Lands: cultural differences which persist to the present day. Despite all efforts to weld the country into a single nation, it retained its duality, and the pharaoh was never the King of Egypt, but the King of Upper and Lower Egypt.

When Sakkara became a royal burial ground, fine-quality funerary furniture and equipment were produced. Since the chief artisan of Memphis was also the High Priest of Ptah, the local deity was soon seen as a patron deity of the arts: the inspiration behind metalworker, carpenter, potter, jeweller and sculptor. Craftsmen from neighbouring areas were attracted to the opportunities for work in Memphis, and its boundaries expanded. Two neighbouring areas were thus drawn into its orbit. One was a settlement which honoured Sekhmet, the lion-goddess, and the other Nefertum, the lotus-god. Combined, they formed the

Memphite triad of Ptah the chief deity, Sekhmet his consort, and Nefertum his son. As befitted the increased popularity and influence of a local deity, priests were recruited from the local population to maintain the temple of Ptah and to accept offerings on behalf of the deities.

According to Manetho, the sacred Apis bull was introduced into Memphis in the 2nd Dynasty. From earliest times animals were believed to be the source of a divine power, a visible manifestation of an abstract force. The Apis bull, revered for its strength and virility, appears originally to have had no connection whatsoever with Ptah, the local deity. As a sacred animal, however, it was treated with respect and left to roam the temple grounds, where it was fed and kindly treated. When a sacred bull died it was interred in a single square chamber hewn out of solid rock on the Sakkara plateau. Another black bull with the characteristic markings (a white spot on its forehead and another near its tail) would forthwith be sought and ceremoniously installed in the temple. The Apis was not yet the object of elaborate ritual; only much later was it said to 'have the likeness of an eagle on its back, double hairs on its tail and the likeness of a scarab beneath its tongue . . .'

The 2nd Dynasty was a period of grave national discord. There is indication of a civil war and the 'destruction of the house of the north' in the reign of Nynetjer, a politico-religious revolution in the reign of Weneg, and evidence of a breakaway government setting up headquarters in Upper Egypt in the reign of Per-Ibsen. This latter rebellion was soon quashed, but it was clear that if a single authority was to be recognised throughout the Two Lands it had to be absolute.

The origins of the doctrine of divine kingship are not clearly understood. It may have been a concept that slowly gained acceptance during the first two dynasties, though this seems unlikely in view of the national instability. More likely it was conceived and implemented by a learned body seeking to establish a state religion as a unifying factor. Aware of traditions, they realised that only a doctrine which admitted deep-rooted beliefs would gain official support throughout the land.

As we have already seen, the sun was one of the two factors that neutralised the physical differences between the Two Lands. In promoting a God-king, who was the son of the Sun-god, the pharaoh was directly associated with an ever-dying, ever-reviving, powerful physical presence widely worshipped throughout the Nile valley. His demands had divine authority on the one hand, while the Sun-god came to have humane qualities of a protective and paternal sovereign, on the other. In other words, the Sun-god was no longer a distant force, but *Ra-Harakhte* (Horus of the Horizon), who had direct authority in human affairs. And the pharaoh was not merely an Upper Egyptian nor a Lower Egyptian but the 'Son of Ra', who was above petty national dispute.

In death, the *Ba*, or soul, of the God-king would take its place beside his 'father' the Sun-god in heaven, and in overcoming death, as did Osiris the nature-god, he became in death Osiris himself, while his son Horus took over the throne of Egypt. In being identified with the chief deities of the solar and nature cults, the God-king became the central doctrine of the state, acting as a link between two separate, parallel but unifying forces.

MAP OF GIZA/SAKKARA

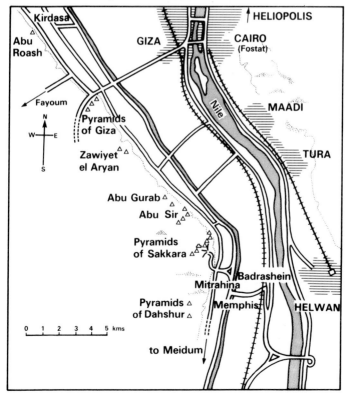

Zoser ushered in the 3rd Dynasty, which witnessed the Egyptian civilisation taking a spectacular leap forward. His name is indissolubly linked with that of his chief administrator, Imhotep, who was also the builder of his Step Pyramid and funerary complex at Sakkara.

2686 B.C. THE OLD KINGDOM (3rd to 6th Dynasties)

Unity having been consolidated, political and economic stability during the 3rd Dynasty was reflected not only in the great strides made in architecture, but also in the active exploitation of Egypt's mineral resources and in increased commercial exchange with neighbouring countries.

Thanks to the painstaking restoration and research carried out by Jean-Philippe Lauer, who since 1927 has devoted himself to reconstructing Zoser's funerary complex, the 3rd Dynasty springs to life, and we can recreate the contemporary palaces and houses which inspired the architectural forms, and theorise on the religious and political organisation of the country as indicated by the structures of the complex (Chapter 3).

The 4th Dynasty was the Great Pyramid Age. Sneferu, who built two funerary structures, one known as the Bent Pyramid and the other as the Northern Pyramid, at Dahshur, immediately south of Sakkara, is the first powerful figure. He has gone down in history as one of Egypt's greatest and most benevolent kings. Under his inspired statesmanship a firm foundation was laid for the political structure of the country, and there was a rising tide of productivity in all fields. Egypt became a centre of commerce. Cattle and raw material, including gold, were brought from Nubia and the Sudan. Power was established in Sinai, an important copper-producing area. A fleet of ships sailed to the Phoenician coast to bring back cedar wood. The state controlled the trade routes throughout the land as well as all the markets. In fact it was the wealth amassed in Sneferu's reign that was so lavishly spent during that of his successor, Khufu, builder of the Great Pyramid at Giza. Within a century from the construction of the first stone building in history, Egypt's highly organised, centralised state reached its climax in a peak of progress never to be surpassed.

On the Giza plateau the pharaohs Khufu (Cheops), Khafre (Chephren) and Menkaure (Mycerinus) raised their monumental tombs. Now stripped of their exquisitely fitted outer casings, they rise in pure geometrical simplicity. Originally each had its adjoining mortuary temple, where prayers were offered for the deceased

One of the shrines of the Heb-Sed Court of Zoser's Complex.

and rituals were performed. This was connected to a valley temple by a causeway or processional avenue. Theories on the purpose and manner of the building of the pyramids date back to the classical authors and continue to this day. Suffice it to say that their scale and durability stand as imperishable landmarks to a period of great technical skill; they were unquestionably constructed on a scale that far exceeds the requirements of security (if preservation of the pharaoh's body was their prime purpose) and oversteps the demands of religious belief by any criteria. Believed to be enlarged versions of the sacred pyramidon or *benben* from the Holy of Holies at Heliopolis on which the Sun-god was believed to have manifested himself, the pyramids are huge and magnificent, yet constructed with the precision of a jeweller. We cannot but marvel at the strength of a state able to promote and support such undertakings.

It has been estimated that Khufu's pyramid alone took twenty years to raise. Those twenty years constantly emphasised a symbol which dominated religious thought and the figurehead who exercised political control.

The 4th Dynasty was an aristocratic era; a period of vigour, confidence and self-assured composure, when the hard core of ancient Egyptian tradition was established. From the intelligence of a family of hereditary lords had come the concept of divine kingship; and from their loins came the ruling élite by the Great Royal Wife, who was of direct Heliopolitan descent. The country was governed directly through members and associates of this ruling family. The vizier, or Prime Minister, who administered the country for the Pharaoh, was frequently his eldest son, who usually succeeded to the throne. The governors in the provinces of Upper and Lower Egypt were selected noblemen, appointed by the Pharaoh. They were given honorary titles and estates, and constructed their tombs in orderly rows on the royal necropolis in the shadow of the pyramid of their monarch.

In the 5th Dynasty, the pharaohs chose a new burial ground at Abu Sir, between Giza and Sakkara. In addition to raising their pyramid tombs, they constructed Sun Temples in honour of their 'father' the Sun-god in heaven. Although the building of these temples and the adoption of Ra as a regular concomitant to the royal titulary from the 5th Dynasty give the impression of intensified solar worship, there appears to have been a division of power between Heliopolis and Memphis. The pharaohs remained of Heliopolitan descent, but the viziers were chosen from the ranks of the Memphites. It is possible, therefore, that the 5th Dynasty may not have been a period in which the priesthood of Heliopolis wielded its greatest power, but one in which the increasing power of the Memphite priests led them to attempt to reinforce the reputation and influence of the doctrine of divine kingship.

The claim to the political leadership of Memphis and to the primacy of its deity Ptah over Heliopolis and the Sun-god Atum-Ra has survived in a late copy of the Memphite Drama, on what is known as the Shabako Stone, so named after the Kushite pharaoh who found it about 700 B.C. This text, apart from providing evidence of the first drama in history, and expounding a highly philosophical treatise in which the heart and the tongue are presented as the organs of creation, clearly indicates politico-religious rivalry between Memphis and Heliopolis. And there is no doubt that the promotion of Ptah as the creator of the physical world was primarily economic; for in claiming that Ptah of Memphis existed before Atum-Ra of Heliopolis, the Memphite priests could claim custody of the country's economic resources.

Memphis features prominently as a populous and enterprising city in the 5th Dynasty. Its main districts were the White Wall, the South Wall, and the House of the Spirit of Ptah with its sacred enclosure where the Apis bull enjoyed privacy and protection. Its riverine harbour saw the construction of many varieties of vessels, both for river transport and for continued trading and mining expeditions, especially to Byblos on the Phoenician coast and down the Red Sea to Punt on the Somali coast. The tombs of the noblemen at Sakkara (Chapter 3) indicate wealthy, influential Memphite nobility.

Division of power naturally led to weakened authority and to the slow diffusion of wealth. Pyramids became more shoddily built with each successive pharaoh, and fell to ruin while the mighty structures of the earlier period survived. Unas, the last pharaoh of the 5th Dynasty, built his pyramid at Sakkara, inscribing the walls of the tomb chamber with the Pyramid Texts (Chapter 4, p. 126).

In the 6th Dynasty the power of the pharaohs was progressively limited. All had their pyramids constructed at Sakkara, but these were of poor workmanship, often with a core of rubble and outer facing only of dressed limestone (Chapter 5). Memphis is the Greek for *Men-Nefer*, meaning 'beautiful monument', which referred to the pyramid of the 6th Dynasty Pharaoh, Pepi I. The nobleman class, however, growing increasingly wealthy and exerting power, built tombs at Sakkara that were large and elaborately decorated with representations of everyday life (Chapter 5, p. 136). Though the quality of craftsmanship had deteriorated, there was still considerable talent.

The enfeebled monarchy, powerless against the growing influence of the provincial lords who had gained power and prestige under them, began to intermarry with them. Pepi I married two of his daughters to a provincial nobleman called Khui, from near Abydos, and royal blood was further diluted when Merenre gave his daughter in wedlock to another provincial lord. There was a noticeable restructuring of society. The exclusive aristocracy that governed the Old Kingdom had ended. Towards the end of the 6th Dynasty the monarchy collapsed and the Old Kingdom came to an end.

2181 B.C.   FIRST INTERMEDIATE PERIOD
(7th to early 11th Dynasties)

During the period of anarchy and bloodshed that followed the collapse of the centralised government, temples were pillaged and violated. The cult statues of the great pharaohs of the Pyramid Age were flung, some to be shattered, into a shaft at Giza. Manetho recorded that seventy kings ruled for seventy days, which may have been an attempt to set up a joint rule at Memphis, but the country limped along in confusion. The Memphite kings of the 7th and 8th Dynasties continued to claim rule for the entire land, but it is unlikely that the provinces took heed. It was a time of discontent and weakness. Mines and quarries were silent. River transport was almost at a standstill. No new temples were constructed. Sakkara was reduced to the proportions of a provincial cemetery. Poverty was rampant and, with few exceptions, the newly independent lords of the provinces were silent.

The Dark Ages were upon the land of Egypt.

When the highly centralised state collapsed it was only natural that this should have a drastic effect, not only on man's political experience but on his moral conduct and religious thought as well. For some 500 years the people had accepted the unquestioned control of the pharaoh. Now there was a restructuring of society, and the very people who had gained power and prestige under the great monarchs began to reflect on the traditional beliefs of their forefathers. It was a time of soul-searching, and great contempt was voiced for the law and order of the past. Some magnificent literature has come down to us from this age of lost values: songs that indicate sorrow and disillusionment at the desecrating of the tombs of the ancestors, on the one hand, and, on the other, voicing scepticism as to whether man's elaborate preparations for the afterlife were worth the trouble.

Some of the provincial lords managed to come into greater prominence in the 9th and 10th Dynasties. A family from Herakleopolis Magna (Ihnasiya el Medina or Beni Suef) wrested the crown from the weakened Memphites (who nevertheless continued to claim royal honours for almost another century) and restored some degree of order. This was achieved by a method hitherto unknown in Egypt: by taking vengeance on all who defied them. Manetho records one of the Herakleopolitan rulers to have been the most violent of Egypt's monarchs. They extended their rule only as far south as Assiut, where their authority was recognised.

In Upper Egypt, a confederation had meanwhile gathered around a family from Thebes. Under strong leadership the provinces had been encouraged to aid one another with grain and provisions in times of low Nile, and towards the close of the 10th Dynasty the leaders started to press northwards. They established a hold over one province after another. By the time they overtook Abydos,

The 1st Dynasty Tombs fell to ruin during the 1st Intermediate Period.

the Herakleopolitan rulers, aided by their colleagues from Assiut, combined forces to face the threat.

Egypt's bloody civil war lasted for countless years. The Thebans finally put an end to Herakleopolitan rule and laid claim to the entire land of Egypt. Mentuhotep the Great faced the formidable task of having to restore order.

2133 B.C. THE MIDDLE KINGDOM
(11th and 12th Dynasties)

The Theban rulers of the 12th Dynasty recognised that Thebes was a thinly-populated province without prestige, and that, in any case, with their expansion of power it was necessary to establish an administrative capital near the border between the Two Lands; they chose a site called *Ithet-Tawi* ('holder of the Two Lands'), near Lisht, situated some thirty kilometres south of Memphis.

There had been total disruption following the civil war. Provincial boundaries could no longer be determined, there were problems relating to irrigation, and drastic changes had taken place in man's moral and social experience. A message of hope was needed to have a calming effect on the people, and Amenemhet I, first pharaoh of the 12th Dynasty, instituted a religious revival. He adopted the title 'Repeating of Births' (that is, renaissance) along with his traditional titles and claimed that he, like the pharaohs of the Pyramid Age, was the divine son of Ra the Sun-god, who would liberate the people from wretchedness.

At first the new state was decentralised. Some of the local lords who emerged victorious after the fall of the Old Kingdom ruled their provinces like independent sovereigns. In fact they claimed that their ancestry dated back to the pharaohs of the Pyramid Age. Slowly an attempt was made to curb their ambitions and neutralise their influence by creating a balance of power among the provinces. Amenemhet carried out a tour of inspection throughout the Two Lands. It was then that boundary stelae (stone slabs, usually rounded at the top and inscribed with texts) were erected. Once there was uniform control of the country's affairs, taxes could be determined and irrigation waters apportioned as a step towards order. Under skilful leadership, the rights and privileges of the provincial lords were adjusted and subjected to the central authority.

Monarchial rule gave back to the people of the Nile valley the authority of a God-king. However, the God-king of the Middle Kingdom could not be a mirror of the Old. The power of the provincial lords and the influence of their local deities had to be embodied in the new system. It is not surprising, therefore, that the God-king of the Middle Kingdom should have been promoted as the incarnation of each of the local deities, being described as a man, a hawk, a bull and so on. Moreover, he became a spectrum of contrasting elements: one who 'conquers by love' yet one 'so terrible that none can stand to be near him'. He was 'one who is beneficent' yet 'the fear of whom is throughout the Two Lands'. He was 'son of the Sun-god Ra' yet also 'son of Osiris, who issued from the body of Isis'. Encompassing the two polarised yet unifying forces, and as recognised priest of all the local deities, the God-king became the successful expression of national unity once again; the nucleus of a united state.

Political stability was soon reflected in cultural and material prosperity. Building operations were carried out throughout the country. Amenemhet III constructed his tomb at Hawara (Fayoum) with a funerary and administrative monument described by Herodotus and other classical writers as The Labyrinth, and more wonderful than the pyramids of Giza. Two pharaohs,

Tax evaders are brought to justice. (Tomb of Mereruka)

34

Amenemhet II and Senusert III, constructed pyramids at Dahshur, the site of the 4th Dynasty pyramids of Sneferu. There was a revival of bold determination in art and a literary breakthrough. Massive irrigation operations were carried out and extensive commerce was resumed with neighbouring lands. Egypt regained its reputation as a powerful and prosperous nation.

With Egyptian influence spreading around the Mediterranean to Libya, Crete, the Aegean Islands, Greece, Syria and Palestine, and southwards to Nubia and the Sudan, the riverine harbour of Memphis naturally saw the bulk of local and foreign trade and was reimbued with vigour. There is indication that the ancient city was splitting into two distinct sectors: a cosmopolitan trading area around the harbour, which saw the introduction of foreign elements, and a conservative area centred on the Temple of Ptah, where local factories produced some of the finest ware in the land. The Temple of Ptah was still one of the most important in the country, bearing the reputation of having attached to it the finest schools of learning.

Though many of the noblemen of the Middle Kingdom constructed tombs at Beni Hassan in Middle Egypt, ruins of a cemetery have been found near the pyramids of Pepi I and Teti at Sakkara. It has been noted that the tombs at Beni Hassan, which were at first large and elaborately decorated, became less imposing towards the end of the 12th Dynasty, and it has been suggested that there may have been drastic measures to suppress the power of the provincial rulers. In fact, at the end of the 13th Dynasty they once again rose against the Crown. During this period of national instability, the Hyksos, a warlike people who had settled in the Delta, organised themselves into a single fighting force and successfully challenged Egyptian authority.

1786 B.C. SECOND INTERMEDIATE PERIOD
(13th to 17th Dynasties)

The Manethonian term 'Hyksos' is a corruption of 'Heka-Khasut' meaning 'rulers of foreign countries'. It would be wrong, however, to regard the Hyksos as invaders who surged across the Sinai and swept into Egypt in a single wave of destruction. As early as the 1st Intermediate Period, when central authority had first broken down, a trickle of nomads had filtered into the Delta. They were content to settle on the fertile soil, at first in small, then in increasing numbers. The restless movements in western Asia during the Middle Kingdom resulted in this infiltration becoming increasingly rapid and the newcomers naturally gravitated towards the centres already formed in the Delta. Soon these 'wretched Asiatics' had settled in camps large enough to cause concern to the pharaohs.

At the end of the 13th Dynasty central authority began to break down for a second time; the Hyksos, who brought with them the horse and chariot hitherto unknown in Egypt, fortified their stronghold at Tel el Deb'a (30 kilometres south of Tanis), moved towards the apex of the Delta, and swept southwards. Their conquest was facilitated by the fact that leadership was fragmented and different pharaohs were laying claim to the country. The damage they did to Memphis and the other cities of Egypt can only be guessed at. Pharaohs of later times inscribed that they 'restored what was ruined' and 'raised what had gone in pieces', but the almost total absence of contemporary documents during the Hyksos occupation leaves us with scanty evidence of what actually took place. Their chief interest in Egypt seems to have been to obtain regular tribute from the Egyptians.

The humiliation of foreign occupation came to an end in the 17th Dynasty, when Ahmose started the war of liberation and finally expelled the Hyksos from the land. Every effort was subsequently taken to efface remnants of their hated rule from the country. The first unhappy exposure to foreign domination left a lasting mark on the Egyptian character. The seemingly inviolable valley had to be protected. To do this it was not enough to rid the land of the enemy, but to pursue them into Asia. Out of the desire for national security was born the spirit of military expansion characteristic of the New Kingdom.

Memphis was now some 1,500 years old. The simple fortification founded by Menes had developed into the most populated and important city in Egypt during the 5th and 6th Dynasties. After the fall of the Old Kingdom a series of inconsequential rulers endeavoured unsuccessfully to keep their city on the political map, but the centres of power had shifted to Herakleopolis and Thebes. During the Middle Kingdom Memphis was once again revived, not as capital, but as the centre of commerce, a highly respected religious centre, and a city of great antiquity and importance. Having suffered the first onslaught of the Hyksos forces, Memphis witnessed their occupiers introducing foreign deities into Memphis: Anath, the 'Mistress of all the Gods', and Baal. For two centuries there was a neglect of national monuments, roads and canals. Though the Hyksos followed some of the country's traditions and called themselves 'Sons of the Sun-god', the Egyptians claimed that they were barbarians who 'ruled without Ra'.

1567 B.C. THE NEW KINGDOM (18th to 20th Dynasties)

After the war of liberation Egypt emerged with a strong government and a regular army, heralding an era of extensive trade and foreign expansion. The military conquests of Thutmose III in no less than seventeen campaigns resulted in Egyptian power being established throughout Syria and northern Mesopotamia as well as in Nubia and Libya. Egypt became a world power, and wealth from the conquered nations and vassal states poured into Thebes (Luxor) where the local deity, Amon (Amon-Ra) was elevated to first rank among the gods.

Whenever a province developed, its local deity was promoted and given wider jurisdiction. In an age of prosperity the priests of Amon were naturally anxious to centralise devotion around their deity to ensure that they remained recipients of the tributes and booty. They forthwith incorporated into their cosmogony the strongest elements of the older cults. They claimed that Amon was the 'First God' who formulated the Heliopolitan Ennead (sun cult) and the primaeval hill at Memphis. They asserted that Thebes was the birthplace of Osiris (nature cult) and that Amon, the god of the conquering heroes, was the 'King of Gods' because he absorbed important nature gods such as Khnum the Ram-god of Elephantine, closely resembled Min the fertility-god of Coptos, and acquired the attributes of Ra the Sun-god.

The people were prompted by the priests to come to the Theban triad: Amon-Ra, his consort Mut, and their son Khonsu, with their needs and desires. Stripped of his borrowed plumes, however, Amon was a national god without spiritual sustenance. The priests had not so much absorbed and assimilated the rich heritage available to them, as taken diverse characteristics and poured them, undigested, into a godly husk with a glittering veneer. They seem to have had no clear spiritual vision beyond the bursting storechests at Thebes, an observation that should be grasped in order for the religious revolution of Akhenaten against the priesthood of Amon to be seen in context.

The size and magnificence of the monuments of Luxor and the impressive military history of the pharaohs of the New Kingdom tend to divert attention from Memphis. However, it was Memphis, not Thebes, that was the principal seat of government in the New Kingdom, and the traditional site for coronations and for important festivals such as the *Heb-Sed*, a Jubilee celebration. Thebes was the religious capital, the burial place of the pharaohs, and the site for annual festivals such as the *Opet*, which took place at the height of the flood, in the magnificent monuments raised in honour of Amon-Ra.

Ahmose, father of the New Kingdom, began restoration of the Temple of Ptah, and Memphis had a new lease of life. Thutmose III's conquests in Asia increased Egypt's prestige abroad, and led to artisans from far afield flocking to Memphis for better opportunities for work. Local factories were pressed to increase production to compete with those of Phoenician merchants who were milling over the city, setting up their own establishments, and even constructing and adorning temples to their goddess Astarte-Ashera. Traders were drawn to Memphis for commerce from distant parts of Asia and Africa, and the riverine harbour became a huge emporium for local as well as foreign produce.

It must have greatly disturbed the conservative Egyptians, who practised their local crafts, to see the youths who studied at the Temple of Ptah during the day attracted to the sacred groves of the pleasure goddess by night, for Memphis had in fact become a cosmopolitan and totally divided city.

The sacred Apis bulls were still interred in separate subterranean chambers, entered by a sloping passage and surmounted by a shrine. Time, however, had seen change in the status of the sacred animal. As a result of the popularity of the cult of the dead during the Middle Kingdom, the Apis bull, like other sacred animals, was believed, in death, to be united with Osiris in the Underworld. The deceased Apis became Osiris-Apis, one of the gods of the dead. A relationship had also developed between Ptah, the chief deity of Memphis, and Apis, which roamed the temple grounds. The latter came to be seen as the living incarnation of the former; a somewhat odd relationship between a sacred bull, originally regarded as the embodiment of an abstract divine force and worshipped for strength and virility, and a local deity, a patron of the arts who had temporarily enjoyed the honour of claiming creation of the physical world: yet a relationship not difficult to appreciate in view of the passage of time and the political, social and religious changes that had come about. To regard the Apis bull as the incarnation of Ptah may have been a natural development to give the living Apis equal importance with Osiris-Apis in the Underworld. Some consolidation of religious ritual and belief was undoubtedly necessary in view of the introduction into Memphis

38

Alabaster bed at Memphis.

of foreign deities with their own priesthoods.

Amenhotep III and his Queen Tiy ruled a country at a peak of its power. It was a time of economic stability and cultural development. In his reign the god Sokar, from whose name 'Sakkara' is derived, appears to have played a cardinal role at Memphis. The seat of power of this deity was on the fringes of the western desert west of Memphis, where the Sokar Festival took place every year. This celebration embodied the most ancient rituals, in which the pharaoh made a symbolic circuit of the walls of Memphis and broke ground.

Amenhotep III's reign also saw an undercurrent of unrest, especially among the upper classes at Thebes. Restrictions imposed on the people by the priesthood of Amon made the state god the target for discontent. Amon was regarded as a parasitic deity who sucked the lifeblood of all powerful cults to strengthen his own, and the priesthood's appropriation of the country's wealth was regarded as political corruption.

Amenhotep IV (Akhenaten) is known as the world's first monotheist. Promotion of a purified form of sun worship and criticism of Amon as a usurper of the "true religion" had their beginnings, however, long before he came to the throne, and continued for some time after his death. In fact, it was following a successful campaign in Asia in the reign of Thutmose IV, Akhenaten's grandfather, that a commemorative scarab was issued recording that he fought "with the Aten before him . . . to make the foreigners to be like the (Egyptian) people, in order to serve the Aten forever". And the symbol of the sun-disk of the Aten was first depicted with a pair of arms in the reign of Akhenaten's great-grandfather, Amenhotep II.

Akhenaten did not, therefore, spring out of the mould of history and make a beginning that was absolute, as is often suggested. He grew up in an atmosphere of internal unrest and foreign influence. He was thirteen years old when he came to the throne and declared himself to be both the High Priest of Aten, the new god, and of Ra of Heliopolis, thereby making no attempt to disguise the connection between the new religion and the solar cult of Heliopolis. However, it was not until he was about eighteen years of age, during the celebration of a jubilee, that he promulgated a decree that henceforth only one god, the Aten, should be worshipped, to the exclusion of all others. He announced that henceforth 'gods' were to be effaced from the land, and the Aten alone should remain. Worship of the state god, Amon, was banned. Amon's possessions were confiscated and his statues destroyed. His temples were spared, since they were too massive to be dismantled, but his name was effaced from the murals.

It was then decided that the Aten should have an exclusive sanctuary; a place where no god had ever been worshipped, no shrines built or sacrifices made. The site chosen was virgin land at a site called Akhet-Aten, or 'Horizon of Aten', now known as Tel el-Amarna. The move to a site in Middle Egypt was as much economic as spiritual. The stopping of caravans of rich offerings, booty and produce from the conquered territories of Asia at Tel el-Amarna, instead of at Thebes, was to prevent wealth from pouring into the coffers of the priests of Amon, and thus to put an end to their influence. However, when one recalls the power of these priests, and its sudden and radical reduction, it seems not only improbable but impossible for a young pharaoh to have carried out such drastic reforms without support. Who amassed partisans throughout the country to destroy shrines of local deities, to break images and deface walls? Since it could not have been the priests of Amon, who suffered as a consequence, nor the priests of Memphis, who had their own problems to contend with, it appears that the only intelligence equipped and interested enough to bring the different cults and the mass of gods and goddesses of Egypt into a coherent system was the priesthood of Heliopolis. It is not without significance, therefore, that when Akhenaten set up his residence at Tel el-Amarna, his palace was built on the same lines as the 5th Dynasty Sun Temples at Abu Sir, and verses of worship to the Aten contain little, if anything, that had not been sung in earlier verses to the Sun-god Ra. The Sun-god of the Pyramid Age, however, was the physical sun, and had ruled a local domain, while the Aten of Akhenaten was the unseen power behind the sun: the single motivating force which spread beyond national frontiers. It was not a new realm of thought so much as a recognition of the unlimited power of the Sun-god; not a breakaway so much as a purified restatement of the predominant religion of the Old Kingdom.

Certain innovations had already begun to transform the character of Egyptian art in the early years of Akhenaten's reign. By the time of the move to Tel el-Amarna, these had become radical reforms. For centuries the reliefs, especially in portrayals of the pharaoh, had been stylised. The 'Son of Ra' was always depicted as strong, powerful and eternal. Artists and artisans competently created long friezes of frozen figures, and were not empowered to improvise. Now, it seems, with the consent of Akhenaten, figures in varied movements were sculptured in exquisite low relief. There was a delightful realism: a swinging gait, relaxed movements, and infinitely tender emotions in representations of the Pharaoh Akhenaten, his wife Nefertiti, and their daughters. The natural and the simple made their mark on what is known as the art of the Amarna Period.

For a short time, a mere decade, religious belief was lifted from the suffocating cloak of mysticism which formed the ethical theology of the Middle Kingdom and from the personal self-interest of the state priests of Amon.

Egypt stood briefly at the pinnacle of its spiritual and creative vitality. But the empire was lost. The neglected armies in Asia suffered humiliating defeats, and by the time the counter-revolutionary forces of the priests of Amon were set in motion, the country had need of a new generation of military heroes to re-establish Egyptian might.

Haremhab, the army general who took over the throne of the pharaohs at the beginning of the 19th Dynasty after the four-year reign of Ay, was the power behind the throne in the short reign of Tutankhamon, the boy king. And the Restoration Stele ordered by Tutankhamon at Memphis was undoubtedly his work. Haremhab started to construct a tomb on the Sakkara plateau (p. 151), but abandoned it when he became Pharaoh, and had a new tomb constructed in the Valley of the Kings.

Haremhab realised the strategic importance of Memphis: an ideal site for marshalling large bodies of infantry and chariotry for his Asian encounters, and he established a barracks there, turning the ancient city into a huge military camp. Thenceforth young princes and the sons of noblemen would be brought to Memphis to learn the arts of warfare.

The priesthood of Amon returned to power. The reputation of their deity was largely unblemished. With Haremhab taking care of foreign policy they were ready to pour their funds into re-establishing the reputation of the 'wondrous god with a many-sided being'. It is interesting to observe that, following Akhenaten's revolution, Amon laid claim to being a 'universal' god also, and many of the stanzas in the poems of the 19th Dynasty ring of the Aten worship. The reinstatement of Amon was accompanied by that of other cults, including Thoth of Hermopolis, Osiris of Abydos, Min of Coptos and Ptah of Memphis along with the Apis bull. And the pharaohs of the 19th Dynasty paid allegiance to them all, as well as to some of the foreign gods which were equated with local gods. Such religious 'tolerance' may be seen also as total spiritual indifference.

Haremhab was succeeded by a series of vigorous pharaohs with an impressive military history. Seti I carried out a series of campaigns against the Hittites, and when Ramses II advanced further into Syria and made a peace treaty with them, the Ramesside building furor had begun. Ramses II, who founded a new capital in Per-Ramses in the north-eastern Delta, did much to restore tradition to the ancient city of Memphis. He made his favourite son, Khaemwas, High Priest of Ptah, and carried out considerable reconstruction on the temple. On his return from a successful Asian campaign he set up a pair of huge statues of himself at its front entrance (Chapter 5) and celebrated his first jubilee there. During his reign several Apis bulls had died, and Ramses II constructed the first common vault for them. This gallery was further extended by his son Khaemwas (Chapter 6).

Ramses III was the last of the great pharaohs. After his death defensive battles were fought to protect the Delta from hordes of land-hungry families who were trying to occupy it. There were labour problems and strikes during the reigns of Ramses IV to Ramses XI. The High Priests of Amon, who had grown increasingly wealthy and wielded great power, chose this uncertain period to seize the throne of Egypt.

1080 B.C. PERIOD OF DECLINE (21st to 25th Dynasties)

Theoretically Egypt was still a united country. In reality it was divided between the High Priests of Amon, who ruled from Thebes (and stressed the fiction of unity by calling themselves rulers of Upper and Lower Egypt) and a powerful family from Tanis, who ruled the Delta. While the theocracy in Thebes became more and more corrupt, the rulers of the Delta showed little initiative. Division of power had once more weakened authority, resulting in a slow disintegration of the economy. Irrigation works of earlier periods fell to ruin. Roads were neglected. Travelling was unsafe. Industry was at a low ebb, and the country's resources were slowly drained by corrupt local lords. There was complete disregard for law and order, and a steady decline on every level. Egyptian rule in Palestine came to an end, and Nubia established independence. Egypt's reputation was at an all-time low.

When the state god no longer supplied a spiritual altar for the people of the Nile valley, and the god-king, the High Priest of

Amon, proved to be no more than a channel through which Amon's divine guidance came in the form of oracles, human values changed once again. Fearful and unsure, and sickened by poverty, the people began to turn for protection to sacred animals, to inanimate objects which they regarded as the seat of a divine force, or to protective deities like Bes and Tauret. Bes was a happy, jesting, bandy-legged dwarf with protruding tongue. Tauret, the Great One, was represented by a pregnant hippo standing upright on its hind legs, sometimes with the head of a crocodile, and with the feet of a lion. Such grotesque deities, often imported and hitherto of minor status, protected the personal lives of the people, and helped them in childbirth and the bedchamber. No longer did they believe that a happy afterlife depended on their exemplary conduct on earth. Gone was the inherent joy and optimism of the people of the Nile valley. They no longer wished to repeat in death their experience on earth. In a corrupt and empty world death was seen as a blessed relief.

A farmer feeds his bull. (Tomb of Nefer)

44

In the Late Period, the poorer classes constructed their tombs on the Sakkara plateau, which is riddled with rough, undecorated, single-chamber structures of plastered brick. Where once the bodies of the deceased had been placed in finely constructed rectangular coffins which in turn had been placed inside huge granite, obsidian or limestone outer-coffins, or sarcophagi, the mummified bodies of the Late Period were buried without such elaborate protection. They were, however, interred with food and drink, which was placed in poorly-fashioned pottery vessels, fragments of which litter the plateau.

950 B.C. LIBYAN RULERS

In these unstable years there was a flowering of a new power. A family from Herakleopolis Magna, of Libyan descent but completely Egyptianised, acquired power and wealth. They were probably descendants of the mercenary troops who had come to Egypt and may have been granted land in return for military service during the New Kingdom. This family slowly extended its authority as far north as Memphis, and as far south as Assiut, thus dividing Egypt into three regions: Lower Egypt or the Delta cities as far as Memphis, the Herakleopolitan province of Middle Egypt between Memphis and Assiut, and Upper Egypt lying between Assiut and Elephantine.

When the Libyan monarch Sheshonk overcame the weakened Delta cities and set up a residence at Bubastis, he proclaimed himself Pharaoh of Upper and Lower Egypt, legitimising his line by marrying the daughter of the last of the Tanite monarchs. He maintained close relations with the High Priests of both Ptah at Memphis, and Amon at Thebes. However, with the priests of Amon attempting to extend religious authority, and the family of Libyan descent attempting to establish administrative control, conditions vacillated between strife and stability.

Under Sheshonk and the nine kings of the 22nd Dynasty a more energetic and successful foreign policy resulted in replenishment of Egypt's depleted coffers. For a time there was a revival of building enterprises, particularly in Bubastis in the Delta, and in Thebes in Upper Egypt. Most of the pharaohs of this dynasty inscribed their names on monuments in the Apis tombs where the sacred bulls, by now looked upon as the living form of Ptah, were interred. Towards the end of the dynasty, the country was again torn by internal feuds and dissolved into squabbling provinces.

Of the next two dynasties little is known. The Delta princes attempted to set up rival dynasties, which appear to have been short-lived. Then a local prince from Sais, by the name of Tefnakht, determined to set his land in order. Step by tedious step he managed to unite the provinces of the Delta, to occupy Memphis and move to possess himself of the sovereignty of Upper and Lower Egypt. Little did he know what was in store for him. For trouble was brewing in the south. Egypt was about to be invaded by the inhabitants of Upper Nubia.

720 B.C.   KUSHITE DYNASTY (25th Dynasty), known since Greek times as the Ethiopian Dynasty

Piankhi came from the region of the 4th Cataract, in the land of Kush. He did not regard himself as an invader, for his people had long absorbed Egyptian culture. In fact he viewed himself as a liberator, bound to free the land from the forces of barbarism. When he moved northwards with his army, he took possession of Thebes, Assiut and Herakleopolis without too much effort. At each of the chief cities he offered sacrifices to the local deities before pressing northwards.

The Delta had already been united by Tefnakht, and in him Piankhi met a formidable opponent. For when Tefnakht had occupied Memphis and announced himself to be High Priest of Ptah, he had strongly fortified the city against invasion. In the face of the Kushite call to surrender, Tefnakht confidently closed the gates of Memphis, which was destined to carry the assault.

The storming of Memphis

Piankhi must have been greatly surprised by the strength of the fortifications of Memphis and by the confidence of its inhabitants. The people refused him entry despite his assurance that all he wished to do was to make offerings to Ptah, and that he would not harm the inhabitants. Tefnakht had, in fact, urged the people to hold on while he himself went northwards for reinforcements. He left plentiful supplies and assured the Memphites that the recently heightened and reinforced battlements would protect them from attack.

Piankhi, however, was not to be put off so easily. He decided on a plan of attack. The eastern side of the city, protected by the flood waters, had been neglected by Tefnakht, and the Egyptian fleet floated high enough for the bow ropes to be fastened to sites in the city. It was here, to the east, that Piankhi struck. He captured all the shipping and, combining it with his own fleet, which he brought to the harbour, he ranged the vessels along the eastern walls of the city, thus furnishing footing for his army. They surged over the ramparts, and within the city walls a great slaughter ensued. The inhabitants of Memphis were finally forced to repudiate Tefnakht and to recognise Piankhi as king. The provinces of the Delta thereupon submitted also. The temples and other sanctuaries in the city were respected and protected by Piankhi, who divided the wealth of Memphis between the treasuries of Amon and of Ptah. After his victory, however, he appears to have returned to Kush, where he died.

Tefnakht waited for the withdrawal of his enemy to temporarily re-establish control of the Delta. However, a decade after Piankhi's retirement, his brother Shabako (it was the custom in Kush for brothers of a ruler to have priority over the sons in succession) marched northwards. He successfully took over the throne of the pharaohs and was the first Kushite ruler of Upper and Lower Egypt. He and his descendants, like the Libyans before them, were completely Egyptianised, establishing themselves as genuine pharaohs, sympathetic to local customs and institutions. There must have been some internal stability during the dozen years of Shabako's reign, for he restored temples in both Egypt and Nubia, showed great partiality to the priesthoods, and when he found an ancient religious text which he recognised as a valuable theological record (the Memphite Drama) he ordered his scribes to re-copy it. The text is now known as the Shabako Stone, and at the end of the text he proudly inscribed:

'His Majesty wrote out this writing anew in the house of his father Ptah-South-of-His-Wall. His majesty had found it as a work of the ancestors, it having been eaten of worms and not legible from beginning to end. Then his Majesty wrote it out anew, so that it was more beautiful than it was before.' (Breasted, J. *Dawn of Conscience*, New York 1933)

Assyrian strength was meanwhile being established, and political events in Asia were destined to threaten Egypt with a new enemy from the east. Shabako anticipated the danger and promptly formed an alliance with the kings of Phoenicia and Cyprus, with the result that he and his successors brought considerable safety to the land, and ruled without molestation from Asia. Taharka, Shabako's younger brother, held his coronation in the traditional manner at Memphis, and strove during his reign to restore ancient traditions, to revive ancient titles, and to build monuments in imitation of earlier structures. Though Taharka was a man of

Scribes in a pillared-hall recording tax offences. (Tomb of Mereruka)

48

Southern Buildings of Step Pyramid Complex. Here New Kingdom visitors wrote of the wonders of their ancestors.

strength and ability, and though he made plans to meet the increasing threat from Asia, his rival was the mighty Esarhaddon, King of Assyria, who had emerged victorious from his western struggles and now directed his attentions to the conquest of Egypt.

671 B.C.   THE ASSYRIAN CONQUEST

The Assyrians, who bear the reputation of being the most military and ruthless of ancient peoples, crossed the first barrier, the Sinai Desert, without much difficulty. At the edge of the eastern Delta, however, their army faced Taharka's forces, composed of local militia and recruits from the Delta, particularly from the province of Sais. The first confrontation was brief, and the Assyrians drove Taharka southwards, where his army were forced to retire into the fortress of Memphis. Either they made little effort to hold it or they were powerless to do so, for within fifteen days Esarhaddon and his troops had scaled the walls. Cuneiform tablets excavated from northern Syria record the Egyptian defeat:

'. . . (*Esarhaddon*) *slew multitudes of his* (*Taharka's*) *men and him I smote five times with the point of my javelin . . . Memphis, his royal city, in half a day, with armies, tunnels, assaults, I besieged, I captured, I destroyed, I devastated, I burned with fire. His queen, his harem, Esanharet, his heir, and the rest of his sons and daughters, his property and his goods, his horses, his cattle, his sheep, in countless numbers, I carried off to Assyria. The root of Kush I tore up out of Egypt and not one therein escaped to submit to me.*' (Luckenbill, D. D., *Ancient Records of Assyria and Babylonia*, University of Chicago Press 1962, volume II, p. 227)

Once in control of Lower Egypt, Esarhaddon divided the Delta into twenty provinces, which became dependants of Assyria. Neko was lord of the city of Sais, which became the most important of the federated states. He was favoured by the Assyrian King over Taharka, who had actually fought his way out of Memphis and had escaped to Upper Egypt; there he reassembled his forces and, less than a year later, marched towards and retook Memphis, driving the Assyrians out of the Delta and regaining the loyalties of the Delta princes.

Esarhaddon died and was succeeded by his son Ashurbanipal, who continued the campaign against Egypt with a vengeance. He drove back the Egyptian army, and Memphis fell a second time. This time, the Assyrians continued southwards towards Thebes and, shameful to say, the Delta princes who had so recently shown allegiance to Taharka threw in their lot with the victors and marched with them as they ransacked the plundered cities of Egypt, forcing Taharka back to the land of Kush, where he died.

Taharka's nephew, Tanutemun, fired by the humiliation suffered by Egypt, and its recent bitter experiences, set out to regain lost territory. With a well-trained and well-equipped army he travelled northwards, doing homage to the local deities in the various provinces and cities he passed, assuring the local population of speedy liberation, and everywhere being welcomed with rejoicing until he reached Memphis. Here he was forced to do battle with the Assyrians, reinforced once more by volunteers from the Delta. Tanutemun successfully scaled the walls of the ancient city and entered Memphis in triumph, making offerings of thanks to Ptah. He reconciled himself with the Delta princes and declared himself Pharaoh of all Egypt. His triumph was short-lived. He could not hold Memphis against Ashurbanipal, and was forced to retreat.

By this time the Assyrians had realised that occupation of Upper Egypt was necessary for the complete pacification of the country, and they marched in the wake of Tanutemun's army. The latter made his escape, ingloriously, back to the land of Kush. The Assyrian army, at last in control of Thebes, plundered the city as they had earlier plundered Memphis. They slashed monuments and buildings, massacred a large percentage of the population, looted temples and carried priceless furniture, ornaments, and even two obelisks weighing 2,500 talents, back to Nineva.

Let it be said that when Assyria conquered Egypt it was not conquering a first-rate power. The Kushite kings, though proud, ambitious and physically strong, were ill suited to the royal role they were destined to play in Egypt. They had emerged from the area of the 4th Cataract to play a leading role in an attempt to weld the tottering nation together, but had never managed to do this. Their triumphs had been brief and they never managed to set up a sound political system. The leaderless and disillusioned inhabitants of the Nile valley had fallen easy prey to the ruthless might of Assyria.

656 B.C. SAITE PERIOD (26th Dynasty)

Egypt was liberated from Assyrian domination by an Egyptian named Psamtik, a descendant of Tefnakht of Sais, who had tried so valiantly to hold Memphis against Libyan mercenary troops. With the help of his Libyan colleagues he managed to throw off the last vestiges of foreign domination and start a new dynasty, known as the Saite Revival.

The conditions of the country were appalling. Apart from the plunder and destruction by the Assyrian army, the lingering decay that had begun in the 21st Dynasty when the rapacious priests of Amon had seized the throne had taken its toll. As their theocratic government struggled to extend its authority, the Priests of Amon had become synonymous with corruption, and a state of semi-anarchy had blighted the land. Provincial lords and their military adherents had subjected the people to centuries of tyranny. Respites had been all too brief.

Though the political power of the priests of Amon had already been shattered, Psamtik realised that one of his most pressing tasks was to render Thebes totally ineffective as a religious centre, and to obtain legitimate control of the remaining fortunes of Amon. He recognised, too, the need to withdraw the rights of inheritance from corrupt provincial lords and to rid the country of a hereditary class. With an ever-increasing influx of foreign elements, there was also an urgent need to guard Egypt's frontiers.

Once national strife was reduced, Psamtik felt he could turn his attention to uplifting the culture that had become debased: where

Unfinished relief of people bearing offerings. (Tomb of Ptah-hotep)

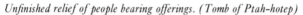

there was more magic than medicine, where art, architecture and the crafts were mere semblances of the original, where religious values had been displaced, and where the ignorant and fearful man had become a fertile field for priestly ambitions.

Against such overwhelming odds, the fact that Psamtik managed to set Egypt on a sound economic basis must earn for him the reputation of being one of Egypt's most able rulers. He first gained ascendancy over the Delta provinces and reorganised a central government, with Sais as capital. He then decreed that his daughter be legally adopted by the sister of the deceased Taharka at Thebes to become the High Priest of Amon-Ra, and that all the property and revenue of the latter should be made over to her; he thus dispossessed the richest priesthood of Amon. He subsequently curbed the power of most of the provincial aristocracy and kept a firm check on the few who still enjoyed special privileges.

Industry was revived, and Psamtik started the restoration of Egypt's elaborate irrigation system, promoting commercial exchange throughout the land. Aware of the economic value of foreign traffic, he resumed and encouraged commercial relations with Syria and Phoenicia. He depended in large part on alien forces for his army: his garrisons on the boundaries of the eastern and western Delta, and in Elephantine, were made up of Egyptians, Libyans, Syrians, Greeks and Carians. The Libyans, after centuries in Egypt, had formed into an effective warrior class. The country's economic resources were devoted to maintaining this indispensable but largely alien army.

Foreigners were so numerous at this time that sections of the ancient city of Memphis were apportioned to accommodate them. The Phoenicians resided in an area called The Tyrian Camp, the Carians within the Carian Wall. The native Memphites held themselves aloof from the foreigners.

A cultural revival under such circumstances would seem unlikely. Yet, looking back into the forgotten world of the past, the Saitic rulers tried to recapture the period in which Egypt had formed its national expression for the first time, and to restore the country to its former greatness. There was a strong nostalgia for the Old Kingdom when the pharaohs had been true-born Egyptians, and the nine consecutive rulers of the Saite period tried to recapture this time by using archaic titles, reviving mortuary ritual, and rebuilding and restoring national monuments in the old style.

Every effort was made to give the government the appearance of the ancient civilization: murals of the 26th Dynasty were copied from the tombs at Sakkara, but though the style was similar the treatment was different; statues were perfect reproductions of Old Kingdom sculptures, but with a certain creative vitality and an added freedom that give them a character peculiarly their own. And official documents were drawn up in hieroglyphics, usually reserved for religious texts. Naturally not only the grammar and vocabulary but the method of writing underwent change with the passage of time. Three kinds of script finally emerged: the *hieroglyphic* writings, which were a development of the pictorial art; the *hieratic* script, which was a more rounded and abbreviated method of writing for official documents; and a further modification, known as *demotic*. The difference between the hieroglyphic and the hieratic is the difference between painstakingly carved or written pictorial writing and the cursive forms of the various signs. Demotic is the rapid form of hieratic. By the adoption of the conventional hieroglyphic method of writing instead of the free-flowing hand which differed with the individual, the texts of the Saitic rulers acquired an archaic appearance.

An effort was made to overcome foreign religious elements by reviving ancient mortuary ritual. The Pyramid Texts were inscribed on the walls of tombs and sarcophagi. So intense was the curiosity of these rulers that they excavated a vast passage beneath the Step Pyramid of Zoser in order to see how pyramids were built, and they inscribed in graffiti that the Meidum pyramid belonged to their great ancestor Sneferu. In fact, it was built by Huni.

Faced with mountains of inherited literature, scribes were ordered to collect, document and recopy the proverbial wisdoms, medical prescriptions and sacred texts. The priests who were responsible for this task, no longer possessing political influence, were provided with revenue. Having to acquaint themselves with an archaic method of writing, they soon became an exclusive class of society. They were not historians, and sometimes in their copies of the texts they gave fresh associations, or rendered them in a form they never originally possessed. Recollections of earlier times had become hazy, and the interpretations were confused; meanings were read into mythology which were their own improvisations.

The unflagging efforts of the Saitic rulers to restore order and prosperity to Egypt, and their stubborn determination to recapture the greatness of the past resulted in their patterning their government, religion, and society on a civilisation that was 2,000 years old. Instead of channelling their energies into the expression of new forms, they fell back on the past. As a result they failed to satisfactorily reconcile the confident values of the Old Kingdom with the passive values existing. For example, the increased reverence for sacred animals, born of fear and insecurity, was totally inconsistent with the confident spirit of the Old Kingdom; yet everywhere sanctuaries were raised to sacred animals and birds: crocodiles, ibis, cats, bulls. Moreover, in blindly copying texts and recapturing traditions, they sterilised creative power and unconsciously thwarted the creative impulse of the nation. They helped to earn for Egypt the reputation of being a civilisation of continuous repetition, void of inspiration, philosophy and individuality. For it was largely due to the retrospective spirit of the Saitic restoration that the Greeks and Romans were later to declare the Egyptians so conservative as to be uncreative, to have a mythmaking mentality, and to revere animals in a manner totally inconsistent with their highly advanced civilisation.

During the Saite period, Osiris, the judge of the underworld, remained predominant, and Isis his consort acquired new and important status. Noticing the devotion of the Memphite population to the Apis bull, and observing that the gallery excavated by Ramses II had long fallen into ruin, the Saitic rulers excavated a new gallery, and inaugurated it for the reception of the mummified bulls. Hearing the wise sayings of Imhotep, builder of Zoser's Step Pyramid, quoted by the populace, the Saitic rulers deified him as the 'Son of Ptah', totally unconscious of the innovation. Thus, in the revival of traditions whose roots had been lost, the results were often riddled with inconsistencies.

Communications between Egypt and the Greek states were, at this time, becoming more frequent. And the Greeks were making their presence felt throughout the Mediterranean world. They had settled in the western Delta, in Sais and in Memphis, and traders and army recruits alike carried back to their land tales of the wonders of Egypt. They marvelled over the monuments of Thebes and they respected the Egyptians' veneration of their ancestors, but the Egyptians themselves they declared to be unworthy of their great civilisation. In fact, the bulk of the population was resigned and introspective. Little wonder they seemed morbid and preoccupied with death.

525 B.C. PERSIAN PERIOD

Egypt's restoration came to an end when the Persian King Cambyses killed the last of the Saitic rulers in a battle, and turned Egypt into a Persian province. The Persians at first respected the religion and customs of the country in an effort to gain the support of the local population. They cared for and restored the dams and canals that had been constructed south of the city of Memphis, and, like the Saitic rulers, they built their tombs on Old Kingdom models, inscribing them with the Pyramid Texts (Chapter 4).

The Egyptians, however, did not take this new conquest lightly. As soon as an opportunity presented itself (in this case the defeat of the Persians on the eastern coast of Greece in the Battle of Marathon) they rose against their invaders and routed them. They managed to maintain independence for about sixty years by forming an alliance with Athens and Sparta, but the Persian army was to conquer Egypt a second time.

During the second Persian conquest it appears that there was less tolerance for local customs, and in the foreign quarters of Memphis the Phoenician temples of Astarte and Baalzephon became active. The Greek historian Herodotus came to Egypt at this time, and he described how Egyptian temples were plundered and how Cambyses killed an Apis bull at Memphis. The episode apparently took place when celebrations were being performed for the installation of a sacred bull in the Temple of Ptah. The Egyptians were in festive mood, bedecked in their finest apparel. Cambyses apparently mistook the reasons for the merrymaking: he asked the officials the reason why the people had not similarly celebrated when he had come to Egypt before. Why, he asked, when his army had suffered such tremendous losses, were they in festive spirit? When the Egyptian officials tried to explain the situation to him, he declared them to be liars who should be put to death. He had them executed, and immediately afterwards ordered the Apis bull to be brought into his presence, upon which:

'. . . like one almost out of his senses (Cambyses) drew his dagger, meaning to strike the belly of the Apis, but hit the thigh: then falling into a fit of laughter, he said to the priests, 'Ye blockheads, are there such gods as these, consisting of blood and flesh and sensible to steel? This, truly is a god worthy of the Egyptians. But you shall not mock me with impunity.' Having spoken thus, he commanded those whose business it was, to scourge the priests and to kill all the Egyptians whom they should find fasting. . . . But Apis, being wounded in the thigh, lay and languished in the temple; and at length, when he died of the wound, the priests buried him without the knowledge of Cambyses.' (Herodotus III, 7–29, trans. Cary)

The reaction of the Egyptians can well be imagined: their hatred for the Persians' uncalled-for massacre of the Egyptian officials, and

56
Farmers. (Tomb of Nefer)

their horror and sorrow at the cruel slaughter of the sacred bull. It is therefore not without interest that we learn that after the Greeks invaded Egypt, only a decade after the Persians had overthrown the last Egyptian ruler, they courted the sympathy of the masses by showing great tolerance for local beliefs, and in the Ptolemaic period the cult of the Apis bull was to reach its most crass form.

332 B.C. GREEK CONQUEST

Alexander the Great conquered Egypt without striking a blow. He made his way to Siwa Oasis to consult the oracle of Amon. There he underwent the necessary ceremonies to enable him to be presented to the populace as the 'Son of Amon', their deliverer, and the legitimate successor of the ancient pharaohs. The priests dramatically related to an eager population, weary of persecution, how the statue of Amon had inclined its head in acceptance of Alexander's claim to sonship, obviously unaware of the fact that Amon's great temples were but empty shells and its priests, totally ineffectual, had become mere opportunists. The conqueror's next move was to lay the foundation stone for his magnificent harbour capital of Alexandria, but he did not stop long enough to see even a single building raised.

After Alexander's premature death his kingdom was divided. Egypt fell to the share of Ptolemy I Soter (Saviour), and under him and the Ptolemaic kings, who ruled Egypt for three centuries until the Roman conquest, Egypt became once more the seat of a brilliant kingdom. Ptolemy I's costly gesture of bringing Alexander's body from Babylon, where he died, to Egypt was designed to give importance to his inherited empire. He announced that Alexander, in his will, expressed the wish to be buried in Memphis. The transporting of the body and its burial gained tremendous prestige for Ptolemy in Egypt. Later, he took the body and re-buried it in Alexandria.

Alexandria had control of the Mediterranean from Greece to Syria, and from the Aegean to the Nile Delta. As a centre for scientific and medical research it attracted mathematicians, physicians, poets, scientists and philosophers. The first generation of Greek scientists built up Euclid's geometry and higher mathematics, progressed in astronomy, built an observatory, and set back the geographical boundaries of the world. Yet it is thanks to the Greeks, and to the Romans who followed, that the myth of 'pagan Egypt' has so long survived.

In the Hellenised and cosmopolitan Alexandria the Greeks were contemptuous of the religious beliefs of the Nile valley, but they were also well aware that their longevity as a ruling power lay in toleration of the local beliefs, and they honoured the shrines profaned by the Persians. They adopted local names and traditional titles and were crowned at Memphis in the accepted manner of pharaohs. Until the reign of Ptolemy VII (146 B.C.) coronations took place at the Great Temple of Ptah, from which it is apparent that despite the growth of Alexandria, Memphis remained a religious capital.

Gazing with fascinated incomprehension at the strange script on the temple walls, the Ptolemies methodically took down all that the 'wise men' of Egypt told them. These were a rising group of priestly interpreters, and many were more concerned with their positions under a ruling power than with patriotism or accuracy. The confusion that had already become rooted during the Saite restoration now became, in some cases, gross misrepresentations. The Greeks were not to know that the once vital nation had suffered cultural apathy: that decadence had long set in and corruption taken its toll. It did not occur to them that the cult of Amon, whose monumental shrines and national temples so impressed them, was over. They faithfully renovated and repaired them, and constructed new ones in his honour, inscribing them with magnificent reliefs and adorning them with statues.

Unlike the Saitic rulers, who had endeavoured to revive the classic culture, the Greeks indiscriminately revived cults that bore no relation to current conditions. Whereas the Saitic rulers had abolished all that was foreign in religion and, in an effort to replace sound values, had stripped it of the accretions of mythology, the Greeks saw mysticism and mythology as basic religious requirements. The Saitic rulers had revived the memory of Egypt's great men, such as Imhotep, and had deified them. The Greeks went one step further. They identified Imhotep with Asklepios, their god of medicine, and raised a temple in his honour at Sakkara which became the centre of a popular healing cult where thousands of invalids made pilgrimage. They even promoted the foreign goddess Astarte as 'Daughter of Ptah', and the goddess of healing.

There is no doubt that the real character of the ancient Egyptian civilisation—nay, civilisations—was never properly understood by the Greeks. How could they understand? They could not read hieroglyphics, and had no idea of what lay beneath the crustated deposits of tradition.

Ptolemy I's most pressing task was, of course, to found a religion

Zoser's architect, Imhotep, drew inspiration from Nature. (Columns of the Temple)

that would weld the two nations together. A common culture was needed to unite opposing factions. The strong resemblance between the early Greek and Egyptian religions has long been noted. The mythology of each points to its either being derived from one or the other, or to there being a common source for both. The linking of their mystical theories was, therefore, not as difficult as would appear. Entrusted with the task of compounding a new national god were one Egyptian and one Greek priest. They found the necessary ingredients at Memphis: in Osiris, and in the newly revived cult of the Apis bull.

The Apis of Memphis was, it will be remembered, believed to be united in death with Osiris, and become Osiris-Apis, one of the gods of the underworld. The Greek word for this was 'Osorapis' which they identified with their own Serapis, and declared to be national god. This confusion resulted in the temple becoming known as the Serapeum. To launch the new deity on his career, King Ptolemy had a dream in which a colossal statue was revealed to him. No sooner did he communicate this intelligence to the people than a statue of Serapis conveniently turned up, closely resembling his vision. It was of a man with curly hair, a benign expression and a long beard. With the aid of a foreign power the hybrid Serapis was to have successes so sweeping that even the Greeks could not have foreseen them. For, launched on a new career, his cult travelled through Greece to Asia Minor, to Sicily and then northwards to Italy and Rome.

Other members of the Osirian family were not neglected: Isis and Horus became excessively worshipped as the Mother-goddess and child. Isis was identified with Demeter, depicted as a stately matron bearing the divine child in her arms, and Horus with Apollo. While shrines were raised to them up and down the Nile valley, the cults of Isis and Horus were also borne abroad, in the wake of Serapis, on the current of the trade routes, to be diffused around the Mediterranean world.

Under the Ptolemies the sacred Apis bull was credited with oracular power. It was said to look into the future and reply 'Yes' or 'No' to questions. It was specially fed with wheat-flour broth, honey-cakes and milk. If it accepted food offered by a questioner, the answer was in the affirmative and the oracle was favourable. The fine temple above the Apis tombs housed different orders of priests who attended the sacred animal, which lay on a couch behind curtains of costly cloth. The site attracted pilgrims, especially Greeks, from far afield. They flocked to pay tribute and to present votive offerings: often small memorial tablets inserted in the walls of the galleries. There were inns to accommodate them, as well as markets and booths where traders sold their wares.

When an Apis bull died, it was ceremoniously buried on a scale hitherto unheard of in Egypt. The Ptolemies excavated a large new subterranean gallery to accommodate massive sarcophagi containing the bulls' embalmed remains.

In the 30th Dynasty a temple had been raised in honour of the Apis. In front of it a semi-circular space was adorned with statues of Greek philosophers (pages 154 and 157) and an avenue of sphinxes joined the two temples. Similar elaborate burials were to take place at Bubastis for the sacred cats, at Ombos for the sacred crocodiles, at Ashmounein for the sacred ibis. Even Anubis, god of the necropolis and patron of the embalmers, became a cult. Thus were the scorned animal cults of Egypt to become fanatical excesses under those who had ridiculed them. Bes, the protective deity of the bedchamber, even became an oracular god like Apis, subordinate only to Osiris, Isis and Horus.

The grain harvest. (Tomb of Ti)

Under the Ptolemaic Kings, Alexandria became the centre of scientific research and the most important port on the Mediterranean. Most of the foreign community at Memphis were attracted to the centre of commerce and activity, and its population dwindled. Alexandria was a Greek city state, however, and contact between it and the people of Egypt was slight.

During the Ptolemaic period an Egyptian priest called Manetho was asked to write the history of Egypt. He must have had access to records, for despite the Greek rendering of the names of the pharaohs, even those of the early dynasties have proved, in most cases, chronologically accurate.

Towards the end of the Ptolemaic period the nation was condemned to impotence by the degenerate leaders who luxuriated in their rich and sumptuous courts and were grossly, even violently intolerant of the local population. The Egyptians staged periodic revolts, but these were apathetic demonstrations and had little effect. By the reign of Ptolemy IV, Egypt began to fall more and more under the influence of Rome, which had slowly risen as a vast power and was speedily expanding across the sea. After the defeat and suicide of Cleopatra, Egypt became a province of the Roman Empire.

30 B.C ROMAN CONQUEST

The drama of the ultimate fall of the Ptolemies and the final conquest of Egypt by the Romans was but another chapter of foreign occupation for Egypt. The Roman domination was a continuation of that of the Greek in its development: public baths and forums in Alexandria, pillared temples up the Nile. The Romans repaired some of the older Greek monuments, built some magnificent new ones, and adorned them in a style that was sometimes more akin to their own culture than to the traditional Egyptian style. Both the arts and the sciences declined.

Though the Romans, like their predecessors, claimed to be the successors of the pharaohs and maintained the appearance of an Egyptian state, Egypt was in fact no more than a granary supplying corn to Rome. The rights of the Egyptian citizens were further restricted, the people were afflicted by heavy taxes and even hunting was controlled by the state. The Romans, meanwhile, with their passion for entertainment, made every holiday or local festival an excuse for revelry, luxury, folly and an excuse for drinking, especially 'Memphite wine'. They carried to its lavish extreme the propaganda of riches and luxury that the Greeks brought to Egypt. The pursuit of sexuality and acts of violence became the order of the day. Memphis saw both oppression and licence, luxury and abject poverty.

The Romans continued the cult of the Apis bull. At a fixed hour each day the sacred animal was led into the courtyard of the temple, a spectacle that attracted tourists, which were numerous in Egypt at this time.

Christianity was established in Egypt between 41 and 49 A.D., when, according to tradition, Saint Mark came to Egypt. It gained a foothold in Alexandria and quickly spread to other towns and villages throughout the country. The spiritual vacuum created when the people of Egypt abandoned themselves to passivity, and to guidance by a corrupt and degraded priestly will, was quite naturally filled by the unified and direct approach to religion offered by Christianity. It was at once more familiar and more simple than the bastard mysticism encouraged by the Greeks, and an escape from the cruel persecution by the Romans. The Egyptians were familiar with the departure of the soul (their *Ba*) from the body to fly towards the heavens, with a heavenly hierarchy and with a salvation in paradise where there was no want. Unfortunately the rise of Christianity was the signal for the rulers' neglect of monuments. There were fanatical disputes within the Church, and some of the early Christians sought refuge in the vast deserts of Egypt, or hid in small cells attached to the tombs and temples. Some hermits chose to live in self-imposed seclusion in the Apis tombs, in the small shrines attached to the various chambers of the temple. Their only contact with the outside world was through an air hole, and they relied on relatives for food, denying themselves all communication with their fellow men. These were the prototype of the Christian monks of later periods.

323 A.D. BYZANTINE RULE

With the reorganisation of Constantine the Byzantine era begins. The Roman empire broke up and Egypt formed a part of the Byzantine empire. Under the Emperor Theodosius, Christianity had become the official religion, and 'paganism' was actively suppressed. There was systematic destruction of ancient monuments. During the two and a half centuries of Byzantine rule a wave of destruction swept the land. Tombs were ravished. Temples were destroyed, or their walls plastered over and repainted with saints and converted into Christian monasteries and churches. Masterpieces were ruined by the folly of fanaticism: a fanaticism not so different from that which had earlier suppressed Christianity in Rome.

The Temple of Ptah was three thousand years old. It had been adorned, reconstructed and enlarged by different pharaohs during Egypt's three 'great periods'. It had also suffered neglect and the ravages of time. At the hands of the early Christians it suffered its first lethal blow.

640 A.D   ISLAMIC RULE

When the Arabs invaded Egypt they brought Byzantine rule to an end and Egypt became a province of the Caliphate. The last official role Memphis played was in being the venue for negotiations between the leader of the Copts (Makaukis) and the Arab conquerors represented by Amr Ibn al As, Omar's general. The latter forthwith transferred their residence to the east bank of the Nile and founded Fostat, adjoining the old Roman castle of Babylon. Fostat was capital before the founding of Cairo.

The Arab conquest heralded a period of further disaster for the monuments of ancient Egypt. The ruins of Memphis were used as raw material for the new capital. What remained of the beautiful polished ornaments from the ancient palaces, inscribed stone slabs from the temples, as well as granite, marble and alabaster, provided quarry for the new city. Ancient inscriptions were stripped from the buildings and the blocks conveyed across the river, some to be used as foundations or reinforcements for walls. Little was spared. The entire city of Memphis, its palaces and temples, factories and fortifications, streets, living quarters, harbour, where people had lived, worked, fought, wept, given birth and died for century upon century, the city that had known the joy of plenty and the bitter humiliation of defeat, was almost totally razed.

Yet so large and prosperous had been this great city, which Herodotus described as having a circuit of about thirteen miles and standing on a tract of land which was fertile and well-wooded, having green meadows and canals with 'their pavement of lotus flowers', that its dwindling ruins could not be exhausted. In the 12th Century A.D., when Abd el Latif the Arab historian from Baghdad came to Egypt, he wrote:

'. . . *Notwithstanding the immense extent of this city and its great antiquity, and in spite of the attempts of various nations to annihilate even its most minute traces by transporting to other parts the different stones and materials of which it was constructed, by demolishing its* buildings and mutilating the figures with which they were adorned; and finally, in spite of the ravages of time during upwards of four thousand years, its ruins yet present to the spectator a combination of wonders which confound the understanding and which to describe the most eloquent would attempt in vain. The more the collection is considered, the greater admiration it inspires; and every additional glance at the ruins is a source of fresh delight . . .' (*The Eastern Key*, trans. K. Hafuth Sand and John A. and Ivy E. Videan, Allen and Unwin)

After this the ruins are rarely mentioned. The Mamelukes neglected the canals, and during the annual floods the silt deposits rose higher and higher, and covered the monuments, until Memphis was a level plain studded by mounds. Then it was to suffer the ultimate fate of all the relics of Egypt: exploration by treasure-hunters who systematically tore bronze clamps from the ancient doorways, smashed surviving statues for hidden treasure, and explored, burrowed and plundered in the hopes of even the smallest reward.

And when they saw that the soil had no more treasure to yield, they turned their backs on Memphis. Peasants built their mud-brick huts around and among the ruins. Villagers at Mit-Rahina and Badrashein planted palm-groves that hid the foundations of the Temple of Ptah, the ruins of the palace of Apries, and the few remaining monuments of Ramses II, Mereneptah and some miscellaneous statues, fragments and stelae (Chapter 7).

What we know of Memphis today, we know largely from the necropolis of Sakkara, the city of the dead.

'Sakkara' is derived from Sokar, an agricultural god believed to dwell in the earth. The Festival of Sokar was an annual event that took place in the 'City of the White Wall', Memphis, at the beginning of the ploughing season. Herds of draft animals would be driven round the walls of the ancient city, as if going round and round a threshing floor, in a ritual to awaken the soil. During the festival, which continued for a period of ten days, the *Djed* pillar, the symbol of the backbone of Osiris, was usually erected as a sign of renewed life.

Since Sokar lived in the earth, the god became regarded also as a god of the dead; hence the adoption of this name for the necropolis, which was the burial ground of Memphis.

66

Restoration of the small temple facing the Great Court of Zoser's Complex (1977)

CHAPTER 2   EARLY DYNASTIC PERIOD (3100-2890 B.C.)

BACKGROUND

Although as early as 1912 a large 'archaic' cemetery was known to exist in north Sakkara, it was not until 1932 that serious attention was given to excavating the site, and another twenty years were to pass before the results were published. It was then established that this neglected burial ground contained the tombs of Egypt's 1st Dynasty pharaohs, and that the monuments were the counterparts of those discovered in Upper Egypt in the 1890's. Which of the funerary monuments was the cenotaph and which the tomb is not known, since all the structures were severely plundered, most were wilfully destroyed by fire, and none of the bodies of the pharaohs have been found.

Today, when 'new archaeology' makes use of aerial photography and statistical analysis, and 'salvage archaeology' rapidly opens up new frontiers while attempting to save some of the world's treasures threatened by dams, highways, and pipelines, the delay in excavating the Sakkara site, even allowing for the interruption of the First World War, is little short of astonishing, especially in view of the fact that the lack of enthusiasm was not in small part due to the belief that they were poor 'collector's sites'.

The excavations of Walter Emery between 1936 and 1956 threw light on the early dynastic period, and revealed the development in architectural design, the high degree of craftsmanship, the artistic skill and fine sense of form that already existed in the Nile valley at the dawn of history.

Mesopotamian Influence

Cylinder seals, and certain artistic and architectural motifs in Egypt which have their prototype in Mesopotamia, raise the question of the extent to which the latter civilisation inspired the former, and of how there arose the doubtful theory of a 'Dynastic-race', the builders of the royal tombs conquering and ruling over the native peoples, the builders of the subsidiary tombs.

Unfortunately, when Egyptology was yet young, scholars were

wont to attribute evidence of cultural contact to conquest. For example, the discovery of pre-dynastic Lower Egyptian-type pottery in Upper Egypt was interpreted as the subduing of Upper Egypt by the tribes of Lower Egypt; evidence of the Horus clan, traditionally settlers in the Delta, setting up settlements as far south as Edfu, was likewise attributed to conquest. When, therefore, such items as an ivory knife-handle were excavated from Gebel el Arak, revealing a style of art unfamiliar to Egypt, when cylinder seals of undoubted Mesopotamian origin came to light, and when the recessed panelling of the first monumental architecture in Egypt showed similarities with that of Mesopotamia, the idea of conquest took root. Like many other imaginative but historically unsupported theories, the notion defies efforts at explosion. To attribute the beginning of dynastic history to conquest gives a distorted picture of thousands of years of cultural development and diffusion during which the settlers of the Nile valley gradually moved from primitive society towards what we call civilisation. There is no doubt that Egypt's contacts with Mesopotamia provoked them to more rapid advancement towards the end of the pre-dynastic period. However, had the people of the Nile valley not felt the growing need to record data they would have remained unreceptive to the Mesopotamian method of writing. Borrowing from another culture is a natural process of culture growth. Furthermore, this type of borrowing should not be interpreted differently from that of 2,000 years earlier when, during the Neolithic period, when Egypt was ripe for the development of agriculture but lacking suitable varieties of grain, domestic barley was imported from Asia.

It is all too easy for the Mesopotamian influence of the 'palace-façade' panelling on the outer walls of the 1st Dynasty monuments to be presented as proof of invasion, without reference to the unquestionably Egyptian origin of the burial customs, or, indeed, to the fact that this form of architecture was used prior to the 1st Dynasty (as indicated on the carved 'serekh' palace-façade on Narmer's palette). Moreover, it is unreasonable to suppose that newcomers to the Nile valley would have had the same awareness of and response to the natural dualism in Egypt, and would have constructed funerary monuments in each of their Two Lands: one in Upper Egypt and the other in Lower Egypt.

Mesopotamia undoubtedly provided the stimulus for increased activity in Egypt. And there is no doubt that as Egypt stood on the threshold of civilization, certain of its impulses were felt and certain of its ideas adopted. But these were integrated, modified, transformed or rejected, for soon enough the highly individual character of the Egyptian civilisation was established.

THREE TYPES OF 1st DYNASTY TOMB

There is evidence of three distinct types of tomb in Egypt during the 1st Dynasty. The first class belonged to royalty or to high-ranking officials; they were large, shallow rectangular pits hewn out of bedrock and divided by cross-walls into a series of chambers. The central chamber was the tomb where the body was laid in a wooden sarcophagus surrounded by provisions on pottery and alabaster dishes, chests and boxes containing clothing, jewellery and games, and funerary furniture. The surrounding chambers were storerooms for various reserve provisions for the afterlife; one chamber was usually reserved entirely for the storage of food, another for wine jars stacked in rows and sealed with clay, and so on. The whole trench was roofed over with wooden beams and planks and surmounted by a superstructure with recessed panelling. The superstructure was hollow and was also divided into a series of chambers which contained the less valuable funerary items. Most tombs had boat-pits for funerary barges.

1st Dynasty royal tomb (Hor Aha)

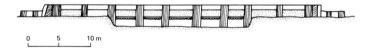

0   5   10 m

The second class of tomb belonged to retainers and artisans. These were constructed in long lines adjoining one another close to the royal tombs, and their occupants were probably dependants in the household of the king, or craftsmen in the various arts and industries. They were possibly buried with the king in order to serve him in his afterlife as they had served him on earth. The tombs are oblong pits or chambers into which the body, wrapped in linen, was placed, surrounded by dishes containing food and jars of wine, as well as the tools of their trade. The pit was roofed over with timber, and the superstructure of rubble was low and rectangular but rounded at the top.

The poorer working classes and the peasants had simple graves, not very different from the predynastic graves, comprising an oval or oblong pit where the body was placed, sometimes on a reed mat, in contracted position and surrounded by the earthly possessions. The pit was roofed with branches and matting to hold the mound of sand and rubble that was piled above it.

The principal materials employed for the structures were wood and sun-dried brick. The wood was cedar imported from Lebanon. The bricks were a mixture of Nile clay and chopped straw or sand. Limestone and granite were sometimes used for flooring, roofing, retaining-walls or doorways.

The purpose of these tombs was the preservation of the body (the *Khat* or outer shell), which was vital for the *Ka*'s continued existence, and the supply of funerary equipment and food in the tombs was to serve and sustain it. The extent of the ancient Egyptian belief that the *Ka* pursued the activities which the owner of the tomb enjoyed during his lifetime is best seen in the inclusion of games and clothing among the funerary equipment and, in one tomb, a grain bin was built into the substructure in order that supplies of bread could be replenished.

The 1st Dynasty royal monuments at Sakkara are, on the whole, nearly twice as large as those of Upper Egypt, measuring an average of 50 to 60 metres in length, and are more complex in structure. Though these ruins are filled with rubble and sand and are not a tourist attraction, they will be briefly described, as they are the oldest dynastic monuments on the Sakkara plateau and they indicate the development of certain architectural features.

Tomb of an artisan

Tomb of a member of the poorer class of the early 1st Dynasty

Interior of a 1st Dynasty royal tomb.

1st DYNASTY TOMBS

1. Tomb No. 3357

This huge funerary structure is the northern tomb of Hor-Aha, identified with Narmer, well known from the famous 'Palette of Narmer', which records the conquest of Lower Egypt, and the King Menes of Herodotus. The substructure is divided into five separate chambers, the central one being the tomb chamber where the sarcophagus was placed. These and the other chambers of the substructure were roofed with wooden beams and surmounted by a superstructure which contained twenty-seven rooms. The outer wall of the *mastaba* was decorated with recessed panelling, and surrounding it were two enclosure walls also built of brick, some dummy buildings and a large brick boat-pit outside the enclosure wall to the north.

The contents of the tomb consisted largely of wooden labels and clay jar-sealings. There were also hundreds of small pottery containers with the royal name of Hor-Aha inscribed on them along with details of their contents. The jar-sealings were lumps of clay covering wine and food containers, and the impressions were made from engraved wooden cylinders run over the clay. These, and small engraved wooden and ivory labels attached to various funerary commodities provide our main source of written evidence at the beginning of the dynastic period.

2. Tomb No. 3471: Djer

This tomb is almost the same size as that of Hor-Aha but is more elaborate in design. The subterranean chambers are hewn deeper in the bedrock, and the tomb chamber is larger than the surrounding storerooms. A vast collection of copper vessels, tools and weapons were found in this tomb, including a gold-handled flint knife (Toronto Museum). The copper ewers, bowls, dishes and jars were worked by hammering, and the spouts and handles were joined by copper rivets. The forms were similar to the stone vessels, which were the chief vehicle for artistic impression; throughout the first two dynasties stone vessels of astonishing technique were fashioned of schist, alabaster, diorite, steatite, marble, limestone, rock, crystal, basalt and other stones. The jewellery found in Djer's southern tomb (which had 338 subsidiary graves for retainers, most of them with crude stone stelae on which the names of the owners were recorded) show considerable strides in the production of gold, fashioned into jewellery and embedding turquoise, amethyst, and lapis lazuli. One of the most important relics of this pharaoh, found at Sakkara, was a wooden label which depicts some festival in which a mummified figure is being carried.

According to Manetho, Djer, who has been identified with Athothis, built a palace at Memphis (traditionally attributed to Menes) and wrote books on anatomy that were copied by later scribes and which survived to Graeco-Roman times (attributed to Imhotep).

Tomb of Djer (No. 3471)

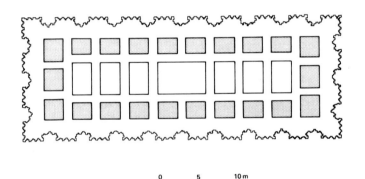

```
0        5        10 m
├────────┼────────┤
```

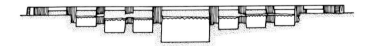

3. Tomb No. 3503: Meryet-Neith

Meryet-Neith may have been Djer's consort, though her two
funerary structures at Abydos and Sakkara indicate that she was
more likely a reigning monarch. Her funerary monument at
Sakkara is the largest and most finely constructed of the whole
group. The structures in both Upper and Lower Egypt were
surrounded by subsidiary graves, many of which were found intact
and contained bodies of retainers or craftsmen along with the
objects of their trade. They are believed to have been dependants
in the household of the monarch: there were pots and paint in the
tomb of the artist, copper and flint tools for the craftsmen, the
shipmaster had a model boat in his tomb, and the butcher was
buried with knives. They may have been buried with the monarch
in order to serve in the afterlife as they had served on earth.

Tomb of Meryet-Neith (No. 3503)

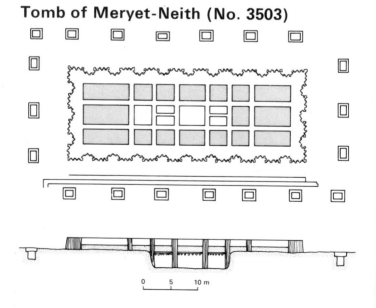

0   5   10 m

4. Tomb No. 3504: Djet

The northern tomb of Djet, unlike the southern one, indicates a definite advance in both design and building techniques. It is considerably larger than the tombs of Hor-Aha and Djer, and the burial chamber is flanked by four storerooms and a further series of subsidiary chambers to east and west. The central chamber was originally panelled with wood which was inlaid with strips of gold plate. (In other tombs coloured reed mats were stuck to the walls in the manner of wallpaper.) The superstructure was vast and divided into forty-five chambers.

This tomb contained objects of high artistic quality, including a funerary stele (Louvre), carved wood and ivory furniture, as well as gaming pieces. The ancient Egyptians were masters of ivory carving, and the tiny lion, the bulls' legs, and the figurines show bold and vigorous technique.

A unique feature of this tomb was a series of some 300 bulls' heads modelled in clay but provided with real horns, arranged on a low bench surrounding the tomb. Outside the enclosure wall were sixty-two servant burials, each with its own superstructure.

Tomb of Djet (No. 3504)

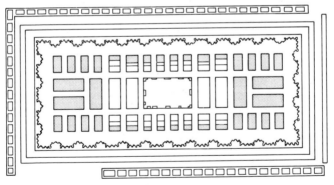

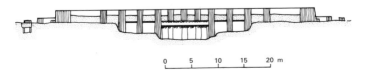

0   5   10   15   20 m

5. Tomb No. 3035: Den

Den's was the most prosperous reign of the 1st Dynasty, and historical documents became more factual: the jar labels and sealings were inscribed with the most important events that occurred in a monarch's reign. These events coincide with mention of an unknown king on fragments of a great stone slab, known as the Palermo Stone, which recorded the name of every king of the Early Dynastic Period, together with the length of his reign and the chief events that occurred while he was on the throne. The unknown king is believed to be Udimu, that is, Den. If this is the case then it is to Den's reign that we may ascribe the first celebration of the pharaoh's *Sed* festival, which will be described in Chapter 3, as well as the 'first occurrence of the running of Apis'.

Den's reign heralds a period of architectural experiment, for each subsequent tomb, as we shall see, shows innovation. Access to the substructure of Den's tomb was gained by a descending stairway that started to the east of the superstructure and led directly into the burial chamber (hitherto the body and the funerary equipment had been lowered through the roof before the completion of the superstructure). The passage was blocked at intervals with stone blocks, supported by props until the time came to lower them down perpendicular grooves cut in the side walls. This was presumably done after the burial, in an attempt to avoid plundering. The shaft and the stairway were subsequently filled with rubble and provided with an outer layer of brick.

The superstructure contained forty-five rooms, some of which were found intact and contained a large variety of funerary equipment, including vessels of alabaster, schist and crystal. Tools, weapons and games were also found. They are the largest single collection of early dynastic objects ever discovered (Cairo Museum). Though dishes and vessels were utilitarian, they were produced in elaborate designs that required carving technique and ingenuity of composition.

The Ebers Medical Papyrus records a remedy reputed to date to the reign of Den.

Two rolls of uninscribed papyrus found in this tomb are the earliest evidence of paper manufacture. Ships trading with the Phoenician coast from early times carried bales of this essentially Egyptian product as cargo.

Tomb of Den (No. 3035)

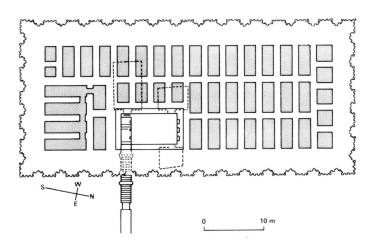

S —— W ⊹ N
E

0 ——————— 10 m

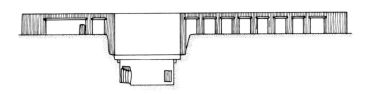

6. Tomb No. 3038: Enezib

Enezib is the first pharaoh to be mentioned in the 'Table of Sakkara' (Cairo Museum), which was excavated from the tomb of an Overseer of Works named Thenery. This list consisted of cartouches of fifty-seven pharaohs honoured by Ramses II, only about fifty of which were legible due to damage to the wall. Enezib's tomb breaks with hitherto predominant architectural features. Over the substructure, a stepped-pyramid structure was raised. It was surrounded by walls of the palace-façade panelling. The tomb of Queen Her-Neith, of the same period and also excavated at Sakkara, has a similar step-pyramid feature within the recessed panelled superstructure. Both these tombs reveal strong similarities in design and proportion with Zoser's Step Pyramid at Sakkara. However, in these *mastabas*, the stepped pyramid was hidden by the enclosure wall, whereas in Zoser's monument the Step Pyramid is the central feature.

Tomb of Enezib (No. 3038)

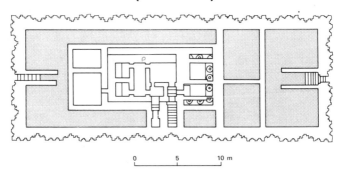

0   5   10 m

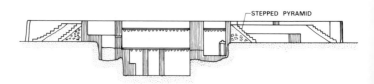

STEPPED PYRAMID

Entrance to Zoser's Step Pyramid Complex.

It is interesting to note that simultaneously with the first evidence of the pyramid structure came indication of a dynastic struggle: Enezib's name, inscribed on stone vessels, was in some cases erased by his successor, Semerkhet (who had no tomb at Sakkara). Moreover, Enezib's name is mentioned on the Sakkara King List, but Semerkhet's has been omitted. Enezib's tomb at Abydos is the smallest and most poorly built of the whole group at Abydos, but Semerkhet's is larger.

According to Manetho, this was 'a time of very great calamities'.

7. Tomb No. 3505: Ka'a

This impressive *mastaba* consists of a rectangular brick super-structure, and is one of four large monuments dated to the reign of this pharaoh, which all show marked progress in architectural design. They have the usual recessed panelling around the brick superstructure, but multi-coloured geometrical frescos were worked on them in imitation of reedwork. In addition, to the north of the tomb but within the enclosure wall is a funerary or mortuary temple consisting of numerous chambers and corridors similar to the mortuary temples of the pyramids of the 4th and 5th Dynasties. The mortuary temples were where the priests effected the release of the *Ba* of the deceased pharaoh from his body. What religious thought and symbolism lay behind the various architectural innovations is not clear, but architectural evolution undoubtedly went hand in hand with religious and political events.

The tomb of Ka'a does not have subsidiary chambers belonging to servants or retainers. The practice seems to have died out.

2nd DYNASTY

The reason for the downfall of the 1st Dynasty is not clear, and little is known of the nine pharaohs of the 2nd Dynasty. Like their predecessors they appear to have had two tombs, one at Sakkara and one at Abydos. The only evidence in Sakkara, however, is provided by clay jar-sealings bearing the name of Hetep-Sekhemui, the first pharaoh of the dynasty, and of Re-Neb, his successor. These were discovered beneath the mortuary temple of the Pharaoh Unas, in subterranean galleries on each side of a central corridor. Possibly their tombs were located nearby. A large brick structure excavated about 125 metres to the east of this gallery has been attributed to Nynetjer, the third pharaoh.

The only 2nd Dynasty funerary structures excavated at Abydos are those of Per-Ibsen and Khasekhemui. It would be fair to

Tomb of Ka'a (No. 3505)

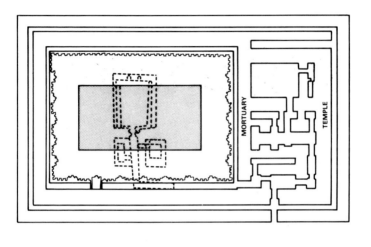

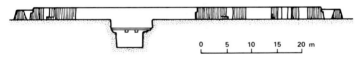

deduce, therefore, that more tombs of the 2nd Dynasty await discovery and that, when located, they may shed light on the civil war which Manetho claimed took place in the reign of Nynetjer, the politico-religious revolution in the reign of Weneg, the break-away government in the reign of Per-Ibsen, and the final establishment of unity under Khasekhemui, who laid the foundation for the astonishing progress of the 3rd Dynasty. Although Khasekhemui appears to have ruled from Upper Egypt (both his tomb and his temple having been found at Hierakonpolis), he may have married a northern princess to consolidate the union. Nemathap's seals show that she bore the title 'King-bearing mother', and since she was revered in later times as the ancestor of the kings of the 3rd Dynasty, she may have been Zoser's mother.

Recently Discovered Pyramids

Three small, or 'minor step pyramids' have recently been discovered. One is known as Sinki, and is situated six kilometres south
of Abydos, another is at El Ghenimiya, a site five kilometres south of
Edfu, and a third is on Elephantine island, opposite Aswan. They
are thought to pre-date the famous Step Pyramid at Sakkara, and
their discovery brings the known number of such structures to
seven.

Based on studies so far conducted on five of these monuments,
they have certain features in common: they are all of solid masonry,
none have tomb chambers beneath them, and none are in a
cemetery. This means that the pyramid was not always 'a tomb for a
pharaoh' as is generally supposed.

The potential significance of these early pyramids is enormous,
both as regards our understanding of their purpose, and of the
method of their construction. Nabil Swelim, who discovered Sinki
pyramid in 1977, explains that markers were used to determine the
corners of the core, the accretion layers and the foundation
pavement for the outer facing. Also, that other markers were used on
the outer side of this pavement to guide the line of connection
between the layers, and a third type of marker controlled the
inclination of the masonry of the pyramid.

Opinions are divided about the purpose of the monuments.
Swelim maintains that they could have served the spreading sun-
cult of Heliopolis, and may, consequently, have been an early
development of the obelisk. A counter argument is that they were
built in royal estates. The interpretations need not necessarily be
contradictory; the 'minor step pyramids', which are widely disper-
sed throughout Upper and Lower Egypt, could have been both a
statement of royal power and a display of its association with the
centre of the sun-cult.

Step Pyramid Complexes and Open Courts

There are two Step Pyramid Complexes on the Sakkara plateau.
One belongs to Zoser (Chapter 3) and the other to his successor,
Sekhemkhet, the ruins of which were discovered in 1951. In both
these complexes the step pyramid is built at the centre of a
rectangular Open Court. There is, however, archaeological evidence
of two huge Open Courts *without* pyramids or tombs, lying to the
west of these structures.

CHAPTER 3   3rd DYNASTY
THE MONUMENTS OF ZOSER (2686 B.C.)

General

Dominating the horizon at Sakkara is the Step Pyramid, the central feature of a funerary complex built by Imhotep for his Pharaoh Zoser, the first king of the 3rd Dynasty. Zoser exercised complete political and religious control over the Two Lands of Upper and Lower Egypt. His reign marks the beginning of the Old Kingdom, an era of great vision and invention.

The Funerary Complex is symbolic. It was fashioned after the existing structures of the state capital, in order for the pharaoh to repeat in the afterlife his earthly experience. All the principal elements are presented in pairs, indicating that all rituals and activities were carried out twice: in the pharaoh's capacity first as King of Upper Egypt, and then as King of Lower Egypt. Naturally the monuments shed much light on the functions of the pharaoh, and the manner in which the distant provinces of Egypt were brought into relationship with the central power.

Zoser's vizier architect, Imhotep, the first architect whose name has been recorded in history, chose to build his pharaoh's funerary complex in stone. Until this time royal tombs had been built of sun-dried brick. Stone had been used for doorways or for the flagstones of a tomb chamber only. Imhotep therefore had no architectural tradition from which to draw, and was obliged to turn to existing forms. He observed the bundles of reeds tied together at the corners of brick structures with heads fanning out, and, transcribed into stone, these became the fasciculated column with capital; he simulated in stone the logs placed edgewise to form a roof; palm stalks, reed fences, matting, papyrus and other soft materials of which the contemporary houses were constructed, and which have all perished, thus became petrified in a medium that lent itself to stateliness and austerity.

The importance of this funerary complex is therefore twofold. It mirrors the structures of the state capital, from which we can glean the administrative and religious activities at the time; and, in faultlessly copying nature's themes, Imhotep, a man of genius, created a diversity and originality of architectural style that has never been surpassed. He bequeathed a legacy to which architecture was to return time and again.

Serious excavation of the site was started in 1924 by Firth, helped later by Jean-Philippe Lauer. In 1932 Lauer took over, and he is still working on restoration today. Much work has already been done, and much remains. Lauer continues his painstaking task of matching up shattered columns prior to restoration. Meanwhile he is also supervising restoration of the Mortuary Temple of the Pyramid of Pepi I (See Work in Progress No. 7, p. 176).

Description

Imhotep chose a suitable site on the plateau of Sakkara and laid out a vast rectangular ground plan of 15 hectares, 544 by 277 metres. He marked the corners with stelae bearing the names of Zoser and his two daughters. Then he erected a limestone wall, over ten metres high, around the chosen site. A large part of this, protected by the sand, was found standing at the time of discovery.

The **enclosure wall** is in the same recessed panelling as the superstructure of the mastabas of the first two dynasties, as regards both the small size of the blocks and the arrangement of the courses. This was, after all, the dawn of architecture, when even the quarrying of stone was a relatively new sphere of activity.

There is only one entrance to the complex, to the east, but there are fourteen closed dummy doors distributed at irregular intervals between the bastions of the enclosure wall. Since the doors appear to serve neither symbolic nor religious purpose, it can only be assumed that they were imitations of an already existing wall, or the ruins of a wall, where there were real doorways; it is assumed that this was the White Wall of Memphis.

The **entrance** (a) is situated in the centre of the largest bastion of the enclosure wall to the east. It leads through a narrow passage, roofed with stone fashioned to imitate palm-logs (now reconstructed), and ends in an antechamber. The entrance does not have any real doors; on each side of the antechamber are huge dummy doors, carved in stone, complete with hinges, in the open position. The door on the right has a slit indicating which panel should be closed first. These dummy doors are a feature of the complex; the same artificial character will be found throughout: only the exterior is fashioned, the interior was filled with rubble. Other dummy doors carved in stone lead to miniature, symbolic, not real chambers; façades disguise no more than the rubble behind

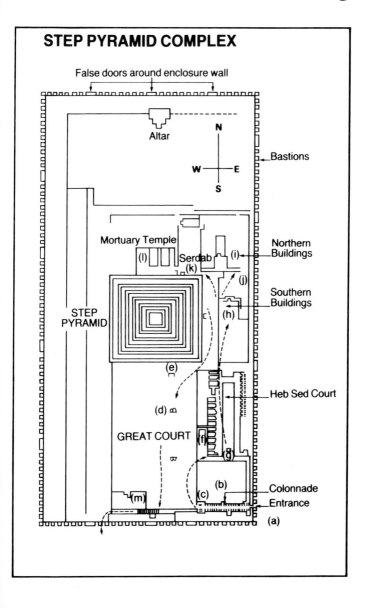

STEP PYRAMID COMPLEX

False doors around enclosure wall

Altar

N

W — E

S

Bastions

Mortuary Temple

(l)

Serdab

(k)

Northern Buildings

(i)

(j)

Southern Buildings

(h)

STEP PYRAMID

(e)

Heb Sed Court

(d)

GREAT COURT

(f)

(g)

(m)

(b)

(c)

Colonnade

Entrance

(a)

them; stairs lead to symbolic entrances, and stone 'fences' separate 'provinces'.

The **colonnade** (b) comprises 40 fasciculated columns, each joined to the side wall by means of a small connecting wall. Certainly, this was less an artistic innovation than the result of doubt about the strength of the free-standing column. The full potential of stone was not yet known. Yet there is rhythmic elegance in these tapered, buttressed columns. They were inspired from bunches of reeds tied together and probably coated in mud with the heads fanning out. The corridor between them is narrow, and the columns show great refinement of line and contour.

It has been suggested that the columns may symbolise the provinces of Upper and Lower Egypt, which numbered about 40 at this time, and that the recesses may have contained statues or emblems of the local deities. The stone slabs forming the roof are protective covering. Originally the centre section of the roof was also carved in imitation of palm-logs placed edgewise. Like the columns, they were in the colour of the reeds, palm trunks, or wood that inspired their form.

At the end of the colonnade is a rectangular hall (c), the roof of which was supported by eight fluted columns which are shorter than those of the colonnade. They are joined in pairs by linking masonry, and have been completely reconstructed. To give an idea of the immensity of the task of restoration, these columns, at the time of their discovery, stood no more than $1\frac{1}{2}$ metres high. Fragments were scattered all over the area. These were collected and painstakingly matched, and the gaps were filled with brick cased in a facing of artificial stone. The capitals of these columns appear to have been imitated from leather skins tied over the fanning heads of the reeds to reinforce them. There are still traces of brown paint.

Leaving the rectangular hall via a narrow passage, where there is another hinged stone doorway open to the right, we enter the Great Court.

The **Great Court** covers an area of over 15,000 square metres, with the Step Pyramid lying to the north. The court contains the ruins of two B-shaped constructions near the centre (d), and nearer the pyramid (e) is an altar approached by a small ramp. The B-shaped constructions may have been symbolic of the limits of the Two Lands, and of the points between which the pharaoh ran his symbolic *Heb-Sed* race in the presence of his subjects. The *Heb-Sed*, whose origins have been lost, is one of the

The colonnade of Zoser's Complex comprises 40 fasciculated columns.

oldest religious festivals. It may date to a time when a chieftain was ritually put to death as soon as he showed signs of failing strength, so that his spirit might enter the youthful successor before it could be contaminated by the ailing body. The festival is alluded to in many of the inscriptions at Abydos dating to the 1st and 2nd Dynasties, and had undoubtedly, by that time, become a traditional festival in order for the leader or king to prove his vigour and his competence to rule the nation. It was a sort of rejuvenation ritual, with celebrations differing in duration from age to age.

Surviving reliefs show that the *Heb-Sed* was attended by representatives of the provinces of Upper and Lower Egypt, who bore their provincial emblems or the statues of local deities with them. One of its main features was the re-enactment of the coronation, during which the pharaoh underwent the ritual four times, each time being enthroned facing a different direction, and at each enthronement having appropriate crowns placed upon his head. After the festivities, gifts of cattle, produce and even personal gifts were given to the various priesthoods before they returned to their provinces. Participation in the festival thus obliged them to recognise the pharaoh as a god more powerful than their own provincial deity.

The **Step Pyramid**, which rises in six unequal tiers, would appear to be a development in tomb construction from mastaba to pyramid. In fact, however, it was started as a simple mastaba, unusual in having a square, not a rectangular, ground plan; and it underwent no less than five alterations during the course of its construction. The ground plan was enlarged and the height was increased in successive additions until, superimposed on top of one another, the steps of the terraced structure emerged in its final form.

The inner mastaba was faced with fine quality limestone from Tura, on the eastern bank of the Nile, and was carefully dressed, indicating that it must have been considered, at one stage, the final form of the superstructure. Successive modifications indicate advances in the technique of quarrying and transporting stone, as well as in the ability to recruit a steadily increasing labour force. For example, it has been calculated that the quantity of stone used in the 4-step pyramid was no more than 200,000 tons, compared with 850,000 tons used in the 6-step pyramid. This economic activity reached its apogee in the Great Pyramid of Khufu (Cheops) at Giza.

Detail of the Step Pyramid showing the original Mastaba.

90

The tomb chamber of the Step Pyramid (1) is at the bottom of a large shaft (2), 7 metres square and 28 metres deep, which lies almost exactly beneath the centre of the monument. It is surrounded by a series of chambers and a maze of corridors (3) to house the furniture and the effects of the deceased. These chambers are adorned with blue tiles, some of them in imitation of the matting that must have hung on the walls of the chambers of the palace, others decorated like a palace façade. A stele, carved in fine relief, depicting the pharaoh striding forward wearing the White Crown of Upper Egypt, was taken from one of the chambers and is now in Cairo Museum.

Access to the tomb chamber was originally by a stairway from the north of the superstructure, which led to the square end of the shaft. A circular opening in the floor allowed for the introduction of the mummy. This opening was later stopped up with an enormous granite plug weighing over three tons. Another entrance was forced by the Saitic rulers of the 26th Dynasty, on the southern face. It appears that the subterranean chambers, which were never

Cross Section of the Step Pyramid

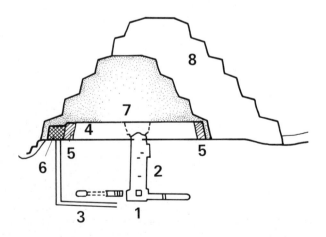

completed, were robbed in antiquity. The chamber at the foot of the shaft was destroyed, and the shaft itself was filled with rubble.

The square superstructure (4) had a core of stone rubble and mortar, and was faced, as already mentioned, with limestone. At this point the structure was similar to noblemen's mastabas of the period, and probably had a slightly curved roof. Imhotep then added a second facing of limestone 3 metres thick in all directions (5), but not as high as the original mastaba. An extension of 8·5 metres was subsequently made east of the mastaba (6), making the structure rectangular, with the longer axis from east to west.

A series of eleven shafts, which may have been designed for Zoser's relatives, led to a 30-metre gallery to the east of the mastaba. Some were unfinished, others were lined with blue tiles and some were evidently intended for the storage of funerary equipment, two being completely filled with stone vessels. It may have been to incorporate them into the tomb that the idea of constructing a second tier first dawned on Imhotep. He enlarged the ground plan another 3 metres in all directions and re-covered the original limestone casing. The height of the two-tier pyramid was, however, still lower than the surrounding wall.

When constructing the third tier, Imhotep included in the overall design a mortuary temple to the north, and various courts and a whole series of dummy buildings to the east. When the fourth tier (7) was raised, the construction could be regarded as a Step Pyramid. The last tiers (8) were added by enlarging a little on each side. The six-tier Step Pyramid, which rose to a total height of 60 metres, was encased in a final layer of fine Tura limestone, though local limestone was used for the rest of the monument. Unlike the brick step pyramids of the 1st Dynasty (Tomb of Enezib p. 78), which were hidden by the enclosure wall, the Step Pyramid of Zoser rose majestically above it. In the 4th Dynasty pyramids of Giza, some of these 3rd Dynasty features, such as the enclosure wall, were to be eliminated, while the bulk of the main monument, the pyramid, increased.

Successive enlargements to the Step Pyramid can be clearly seen on the south, north and eastern faces. At the north-eastern corner the third mastaba can be seen where the facing has fallen away. The base of the casing of the first mastaba can be seen against it.

Crossing the Great Court diagonally towards the east, we come to a small rectangular temple (f), which is in process of reconstruction. It was from this point that the Pharaoh emerged to take part in the *Heb-Sed* Festivities.

Following the circular wall to the right, we enter the **Heb-Sed Court**. This court is rectangular and flanked by shrines to the east and the west. These were designed to house the statues of the deities of the provinces of Upper and Lower Egypt, borne by representatives of each. The shrines face the court, and each has a dummy door in open position leading to a tiny chamber with a niche. A wall decorated with 'reed-barrier' fences separates each 'province' from the next.

The façades of the shrines are not uniform. The first and last on the left, for example, have the square shape with projections at the top which later became widely used in Egyptian monuments. The other shrines on the left have curved cornices and are decorated with three small engaged crenellated columns, the tops of which have unusual ornamental pendant leaves. The holes between the leaves may have held flags or emblems of the various provinces, and undoubtedly each niche once held a statue of a local deity. The last shrine on the right of the court combines the architectural features, having a curved cornice with side projections.

We cannot but marvel at the pure lines and perfect proportion of the façades of these shrines, especially when we recall that this was the dawn of architecture. Imhotep did not invent the forms; he transcribed existing forms, accounting for their diversity. And, moreover, since these were symbolic structures, never to be used by man, it was not necessary to create bulk for strength. Thus the semblance of the lightness of nature's forms have not been lost in stone.

The square platform (g) was probably a reproduction of the one on which the pharaoh, in his capital, was seated on a throne and underwent his symbolical crowning ceremonies in the presence of his subjects.

Towards the end of the *Heb-Sed* Court, on the left, are four unidentified pairs of feet on a pedestal, which now has a protective covering.

North of the *Heb-Sed* Court is another spacious court and the **Southern Buildings** (h) with a façade of engaged crenellated columns supporting a cornice which follows the curve of the roof. For a nation that prided itself on symmetry and balance, the entrance is surprisingly situated between the 2nd and 3rd columns. The entrance leads to a narrow passage, a small chamber and three niches. On the left of the entrance and facing the doorway are graffiti inscribed in hieratic, the cursive form of hieroglyphics. These are the earliest records of tourists. They date from the New

Kingdom, when Upper Egyptians from Thebes came to Sakkara and marvelled at their ancestors' monuments, then well over a thousand years old. Their comments (protected by glass) indicate wonder and admiration for 'Zoser'; this is the first instance of the pharaoh Neter-Khet ('Divine Body': his traditional Horus name), being referred to by his other name, Zoser.

Situated at the end of a small courtyard to the north are the **Northern Buildings** (i), which are similar in appearance to the southern. To the east of the entrance are three engaged columns (j) fashioned in the form of the papyrus plant. These delicate columns so accurately simulate nature that the triangular stem can be clearly seen, thickening at a point just above the ground, and slimming towards the fanning head of the plant.

The **Serdab** (k) is situated on the northern face of the pyramid. This is a special chamber into which the statue of the deceased, sculpted to look exactly like him, was placed. This statue was regarded as the seat of his *Ka*, which would see the offerings and smell the burning incense through two small round holes, which were the only openings. The statue in the *Serdab* is a cast of the

Engaged papyrus columns near the Northern Buildings of Zoser's Complex.

original, which is in Cairo Museum.

The **Mortuary Temple** (l) is also situated on the northern face of the pyramid. It is largely in ruin. Only the base of the columns and the outline of the courts can be seen. However, it has been observed that the courts, as well as the ablution chambers and the recesses, are all built in pairs. Since it was in the Mortuary Temple that priests prayed for the release of the *Ba* or soul of the deceased to heaven, it is clear that the dual monarchy, which is apparent from the other structures of the complex, was repeated in the rituals for the afterlife. The complex of Zoser therefore contains a *Serdab* with a statue for housing the *Ka*, which partook of offerings, and a mortuary temple for the release of the *Ba* to heaven; and in the tomb chamber beneath the pyramid was the mummified body, the *Khat*, which was also the repository for the *Ka*.

As already mentioned, the original entrance to the tomb chamber was on the northern face, running from the Mortuary Temple, through a trench, then through a tunnel, and ending in the roof at the foot of the shaft above the tomb chamber. Entrances to pyramids were generally on the north, where Sothis, the Dog-Star, rose just before sunrise between July 19th and 20th each year, marking the beginning of the Solar Year. This phenomenon, observed in Memphis, heralded the rising of the Nile flood, which was a sign of rebirth.

Southern Tomb: Retracing our footsteps across the Great Court we approach a right-angled projection in the southwest corner of the court (m). This seemingly solid masonry is a sanctuary or storeroom, accessible from the outside of the enclosure wall only. At the top of the projection is a fine frieze of *uraei* (cobra), the emblem of the province of Buto, capital of the Delta Kingdom before unification. Below the frieze is a finely panelled wall.

Mounting the steps to the top of the enclosure wall one can look down a 28-metre shaft leading to a second tomb chamber. This is smaller than that under the pyramid, and was discovered two years before entry was made into the tomb chamber beneath the pyramid.

Access to this chamber is by a sloping tunnel (closed to the public) leading to a shaft and a series of small connecting galleries lined with blue tiles. The chamber above the tomb chamber contained a large granite plug. In other words these galleries and chambers are exactly the same as those under the Step Pyramid. Three stelae bearing the figure of Zoser in low relief were found here. In one representation he strides forward wearing the Red Crown. In the other he is depicted standing, with the White Crown on his head. The striding figure, too, is similar to that found beneath the Step Pyramid. The only difference, in fact, is that the tomb chamber is much smaller, measuring a mere 1·58 metres in length. Since this is too small for an average person, one must assume that the tomb chamber beneath the pyramid was where the body of Zoser was buried, and that this chamber was for some other purpose. There are two possibilities. One is that it may have been intended for the vital organs of the King, which had been removed from the body and buried separately (later such organs were stored in containers in a Canopic Chest placed in the tomb chamber with the coffin). Or it may have represented the cenotaph which the earlier pharaohs had had erected near Abydos, in Upper Egypt, and which Zoser, a Lower Egyptian, decided to have within the Funerary Complex.

Apart from some 40,000 alabaster and diorite vessels, inscribed with the names of earlier kings and officials, the contents of the subterranean chambers in the complex, including the eleven for the royal family, had been ruthlessly plundered. In one of the two alabaster sarcophagi found in the royal family tombs, a coffin was discovered, containing the mummy of a child. The other was empty but had been embossed in gold which had been ripped off by robbers.

In 1934 Lauer discovered a mummified foot in the granite chamber beneath the pyramid. The body of Zoser had long disappeared from its final resting place, but this foot, mummified in the manner of the early dynasties, may well be the last relic of one of Egypt's great pharaohs. It is now at the Faculty of Medicine, Cairo University.

Search for the Tomb of Imhotep

The tomb of Imhotep, vizier of the pharaoh Zoser and venerated much later as a god of medicine, has not yet been found. Walter Emery, working for the Egypt Exploration Society, conducted an excavation between 1965 and 1970 in search of it. He chose a site in north Sakkara, west of the 3rd Dynasty tombs, which was believed to be the centre of a popular healing cult in later times. His dig revealed shaft burials and a network of underground catacombs dating to Graeco-Roman times. Mummified ibises and hawks were found stacked from rock-bed to ceiling. The ibis birds were encased in clay jars, some of their wrappings were beautifully decorated with the images of deities. He also found shafts containing mummified baboons and a cemetery of cows, which were the mothers of the sacred Apis bulls; one skull was intact, in a decorated clay plaster casing.

After Emery's death, Professor Harry S. Smith classified his material in preparation for publication, and also began a survey of north Sakkara, from the Pyramid of Teti to Abu Sir.

TOMB OF HESI-RA (not accessible to Tourists)

The tomb of this important 3rd Dynasty nobleman lies at the northern end of the necropolis. It is distinguished by two long painted brick corridors, the inner one of which is recessed. One wall is decorated with a blaze of colour; variegated mat patterns were painted on to the panelled mud-brick wall in much the manner of the blue tiles of Zoser's tomb chamber, and similarly framing the carved wooden panels that were situated to the rear of each of the niches. On the opposite wall, the deceased's funerary furniture was realistically depicted. Some badly damaged scenes of men and cattle waiting at a canal, and of a crocodile in the water, are the earliest scenes of everyday life depicted on tomb walls.

The wooden panels (Cairo Museum) are carved in low relief and depict the deceased either standing, in various attitudes, or seated before a table of offerings. They are examples of the superb quality of relief sculpture at an early period. They are bold in conception and vigorous in execution. This was a period in which traditions were being established. Egyptian art was not rigid, and not yet subject to mass production by funerary workshops.

Representations of Hesi-Ra's funerary furniture, fashioned with delicacy and skill, included chairs and beds of wood decorated with copper fittings, leather seats and thongs for the beds, and the chair legs carved in the form of the fore and hind legs of bulls.

The household furnishings and objects from this tomb, as well as the representations on the panels, indicate a luxurious standard of living.

TOMB OF KA-APERU

This tomb, built of crude brick and with a door of limestone, is an early and simple type, consisting of one single chamber. It is of interest because it was here that one of the most famous and beautiful statues of the Old Kingdom was found, by Mariette. It is now in the Cairo Museum and is known as the 'Sheikh el Beled' or 'village chief'. By strange coincidence the statue of Ka-Aperu was so like the sheikh of the village that the workers excavating the chamber, immediately on extracting it from the sand, shouted the name by which it is still known.

The statue, fashioned in wood, shows a heavy, broadly built, well-fed but energetic man striding forward, with an acacia staff in his hand. His wide open eyes are uncannily real, and the hollowed sockets hold black and white enamel eyes with copper marking the outlines of the lids. Inserted at the back of the pupils are tiny polished metal knobs used both to secure the eye in position and, at the same time, to give it the sparkle of a living glance.

Although the pedestal and the legs of the statue had decayed (they have now been restored), the statue was found in an upright position, held firmly thus by the surrounding sand. The head, torso and arms were intact.

STATUARY

To conduct a tourist through an empty tomb, and to ignore the question of statuary because almost all of the statues have been removed for safe-keeping, would be to fall short of representing a true picture of this vital period of the ancient Egyptian civilization. For the hundreds of statues of the Old Kingdom, like the wall reliefs of the tombs, have a great deal to tell us. In fact the reliefs themselves may be regarded as an accompaniment of, or a substitute for, sculpture. And the sculpture forms undoubtedly influenced the low reliefs. Both were painted.

The 'Sheikh el Beled' himself was originally covered with lime and coated with plaster which was then coloured. Even statues of stone, which had natural tints, were subjected to additional tinting. Sculptors were ambitious in their use of materials, fashioning statues of stone, wood and metal.

The statues, like the reliefs of the tombs from which they come, reflect the confidence and well-being of the people of the Old Kingdom. The statue of Nofir, the Director of the Granaries, is one of the finest examples of the period (Cairo Museum), showing an obvious, if perhaps unconscious, realism. And every statuette of a common man can find its parallel in the wall reliefs, not only in the activities themselves, but in the very attitudes and movements: a naked peasant going to market with his sandals in his hand and his bag slung over his shoulder, a baker and his wife kneading dough, scribes recording produce, or a female figure walking with a basket on her head.

The statue of the dwarf Khnum-Hotep (left) is modelled in refined detail, with sturdy legs and corpulent body. He was a storekeeper. In some tombs dwarfs are depicted fashioning jewellery, and it has been suggested that physically handicapped people may have been employed in such places because of their inability to flee if a theft occurred!

The portrait sculptor of the Old Kingdom was the greatest artist of the age. This uninscribed head of a noblewoman (below), unofficially labelled as 'Madame Sheikh el Beled', is a masterpiece of realism. Sometimes a lifelike effect was given to the face by inserting pieces of quartz in the eye sockets with a copper stud, which served also as the pupil.

One of the few statues preserved intact in a tomb is that of Mereruka (opposite), where he is sculpted walking forward, out of his tomb, into the sacrificial chamber, to partake of offerings. The reason why the statue survived in situ is because the tomb was covered in sand in Graeco–Roman times when the Serapeum Way (p. 154) was constructed, and, unaware of what lay beneath, the builders laid down the paving stones above the standing statue, thus protecting it.

The statue of Mereruka shows a vigorous man walking forward.

CHAPTER 4   5th DYNASTY
(2494-2345 B.C.)

MASTABAS
General

The earliest *mastabas* contained a single chamber which was inaccessible from without. The body of the deceased, along with the funerary equipment, was lowered through the roof before the completion of the superstructure. A door-shaped stele, set in a shallow recess on the outside of the eastern wall, was regarded as the entrance to the tomb and, in front of it, on a flat sacrificial slab, the relatives of the deceased placed food, drink and other offerings.

Later, when access to the tomb chamber was made from outside the superstructure, offerings could be made within the funerary chamber of the mastaba in front of the stele, which was now placed on the western wall. The stele was regarded as the symbolic entrance to the tomb. Behind it a perpendicular shaft led directly into the rock-hewn burial chamber where the body, crudely wrapped in bandages, lay in a wooden or stone coffin. After it had been lowered, the shaft was filled with sand, but the *Ka* of the deceased could pass through the shaft and the false door into the funerary chamber, and inhabit the statue of the deceased in the *Serdab* (the Arabic word for 'cellar').

Mummification had not been perfected in the Old Kingdom (see Chapter 7 p. 159), and to safeguard against the possibility of annihilation should the body perish and the *Ka* have nowhere in which to repose, an alternative was provided: a statue of the deceased, sculpted to look exactly like him in the vigour of youth. The *Serdab* was built into the thickness of the wall designed to give the maximum protection to the statue. The only connection with the outer chamber were tiny slits in the masonry through which the *Ka*, inhabiting the statue, could witness the offerings and ceremonies. As a further insurance against annihilation should the statue, despite the protection, be damaged or destroyed, several statues were often fashioned, and more than one *Serdab* provided in a single mastaba. When progress was made in the art of mummification during the Middle Kingdom, the *Serdab* and the statues fell into disuse.

This copy of a statue of Ti in the Serdab *is visible through a slit in the masonry.*

Though it was the duty of relatives of the deceased to continue to supply offerings, naturally some laxity was to be expected with the passage of time. As early as the 2nd Dynasty funerary stelae were introduced in the tombs. These were carved with scenes of the deceased before a table of food, and the accompanying text declared that he had received sufficient daily offerings. By the 4th and 5th Dynasties, when the noble class possessed large material assets, they instructed their artists to depict lists of offerings alongside the traditional table of offerings. Such scenes, which were believed to serve in place of the real thing, did not mean that fresh food was no longer considered necessary. On the contrary, a wealthy nobleman bequeathed some of his land to priests, the revenue of which was for the maintenance of the tomb and the continued provision of fresh offerings.

Towards the end of the Old Kingdom, when the noblemen had become extremely wealthy, their mastabas were enlarged and the number of storerooms increased. Some of the mastabas at Sakkara have series of chambers for the nobleman himself, his wife, and his son.

The ancient Egyptians believed that the afterlife was an extension of their earthly experience. Wishing to ensure bounty in the afterlife similar to that enjoyed on earth, they depicted in their tombs a wide variety of farming scenes, manufacturing processes and leisure activities as well as scenes from their personal lives. The walls of the mastabas were divided into different registers, and all available wall-space was decorated with reliefs of men, women, children, birds and animals. There are similar scenes in many tombs, indicating a common stock of themes from which a nobleman might take his choice, but no two scenes are exactly alike. There is endless variety.

The rich depiction on the walls of the noblemen's tombs gives a realistic and appealing picture of the daily lives of the people: the deceased himself, his wife and children, the overseers of his estates and factories, the scribes, working classes and peasants. Also carved in relief are short explanatory texts of the actions depicted, often in the form of a commentary. These mastabas are the main source of our knowledge of daily life in ancient Egypt during the Old Kingdom.

TOMB OF TI (Court Dignitary)

Ti's tomb is unrivalled for its variety of detailed representations of life in ancient Egypt. It was first excavated by Mariette in 1865 and has been restored by the Egyptian Department of Antiquities. The tomb, now somewhat sunken in the sand, once stood at ground level. It comprises a small entrance (1) containing two square pillars, a spacious open court surrounded by square pillars (2), in the centre of which is a flight of stairs (3), leading to a subterranean passage extending the full length of the structure and ending in an antechamber and tomb chamber. The sarcophagus completely fills the niche in which it stands. It was empty when found. The corridor (4) extends from the right of the rear wall and leads to a side chamber (5), the funerary chamber (6) and the *Serdab* (7).

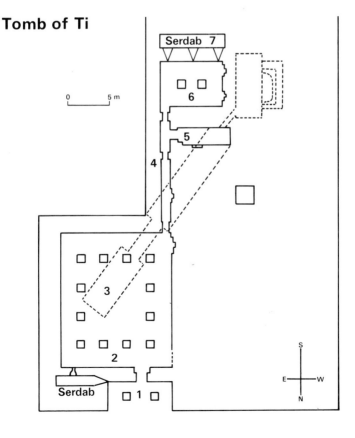

Tomb of Ti

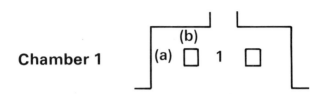

Chamber 1

Chamber 2

Description

On the descent to the entrance (1), vigorous relief portraits of the deceased nobleman can be seen against the square pillars at the threshold of his tomb. He leans on a staff and the inscription informs us that he served under three pharaohs. His titles include Overseer of the Pyramids and Sun Temples at Abu Sir, Supervisor of Works, Scribe of the Court, and Royal Councillor. He was so highly regarded by his pharaoh that he became a special confidant, bearing the title Lord of Secrets (of the pharaoh), and a princess, Nefer-Hotep-S, was given to him as wife. His children ranked as royalty.

Most of the reliefs at the entrance have been destroyed, apart from the left-hand wall (a), where peasants, representing the villages belonging to Ti, bear food in a procession. The rear left-hand wall (b) shows the deceased with his son. There are also some poultry scenes, and doves being fattened.

Passing through the doorway we enter the Court (2). The twelve pillars (only one of which bears the figure of the deceased nobleman) once supported a roof. Unfortunately the walls have been long exposed and are much faded. However, at (c) is a scene of overthrowing of an ox, and its slaughter, watched by the deceased and his son. The animal's hind legs and one front leg are roped in order to throw it. At (d) Ti is being borne in a carrying-chair, preceded by attendants bearing fans, boxes and chairs. One attendant leads the nobleman's pets: a greyhound and a monkey.

On the right-hand wall are a series of scenes showing Ti (e) carrying a long staff, accompanied by his wife, inspecting the forced feeding of cranes and geese. A man fans the fire beneath a copper pot; another holds an object over the steam. At (f) Ti and his wife inspect a poultry yard. Note the realism with which the fowl are carved in extremely low relief. At (g) Ti receives accounts from his officials. They stand in a structure supported by columns. In a series of representations we can follow a scribe's arrival and the various movements he makes in front of the nobleman: a forward stride, a short bow, opening the papyrus roll, and reading the records.

On each side of the doorway leading to the inner chambers there are three representations of Ti. Each depicts him walking out of the tomb, and each figure is clad in a different costume, indicating his various administrative functions. The central figures are clad in the panther skin of a High Priest. The heads of noblemen were usually cropped, and they wore different wigs. The linen kilt-like skirt, either knee or mid-calf length, was starched and secured by a girdle around the waist. The collar, encrusted with semi-precious stones, was worn on the bare torso. Sometimes leather bands were worn across the chest.

In the corridor (4), the reliefs are in a much better state of preservation. In the first half, the walls carry the traditional offering scenes in all the registers. Servants bear these in the four basic forms: liquid, solid, dead and alive. Note the wide variety of different positions in which the geese are carried, and the fine manner in which the animals are carved. The stele on the right is dedicated to Ti's wife.

The corridor extends beyond the doorway, where the reliefs are in extremely good condition. The original colours are still bright. The lower register of the left-hand wall (h) shows the slaughter of cattle for sacrifice. From left to right: two men carry bowls which were probably for collecting the blood, a third man sharpens his knife with a flint tied to the end of his apron. In the next representation he begins to dismember the animal and tucks the flint safely away in the back of his belt. In the next, he again sharpens it until all the limbs have been removed. These are carried towards the funerary chamber.

In the second register (from left to right) is a scene depicting the transporting of statues on sledges. Water is poured on the earth just in front of the sledge. Since the surface of wet Nile clay is extremely slippery, this enabled the wooden sledge to be drawn more easily. Two men behind the sledge bear the surplus water.

In the upper register a seated statue is being towed in similar manner.

On the right-hand wall (i) is a series of representations of sailing vessels. One unique ship is shown in full sail. In place of a rudder, a man-manipulated oar was used. Note the lively attitudes of the sailors.

Above the doorway through which we have just passed (j) Ti and his wife are shown on an outing through the marshes. They sail in a papyrus skiff.

Above the doorway opposite (k), Ti, with his wife seated at his feet, is entertained by an orchestra. They listen (from left to right) to a flautist, two singers, two harpists and a singer. One of the singers holds his hand cupped behind his ear to give resonance to his voice: this is still the practice in Upper Egypt where the double flute is still used. In the lower two registers there are dancers and, to the extreme right, women clap their hands for rhythm.

Stairway leading to the burial chamber. (Tomb of Ti)

The doorway to the right leads to a small chamber (5) which was probably a storeroom, and most of the scenes show offerings. On the right-hand wall, at (l), Ti receives flowers, pastry and poultry from servants. Above the niche are different varieties of bread in many shapes. On the rear wall (m) there are representations of baking and brewing, with the learned scribes making careful note of the quantities. The left-hand wall (n) also contains scenes of gift-bearers and offerings, and above the doorway are stylised representations of low tables laden with vessels of various shapes and sizes. Hieroglyphic texts itemise 'sixteen kinds of bread and cakes, six kinds of wine, and four kinds of beer'.

Chamber (6) is the sacrificial chamber, which is richly adorned and preserved. The two large square pillars are covered with stucco and painted to imitate red granite. They bear the names and titles of Ti, whose figure dominates all the scenes. He is the lord of the estate, buried in the tomb chamber, and in order to ensure a repetition in the afterlife of his experiences on earth, he ordered his artists to decorate the walls of his tomb with a wide variety of activities.

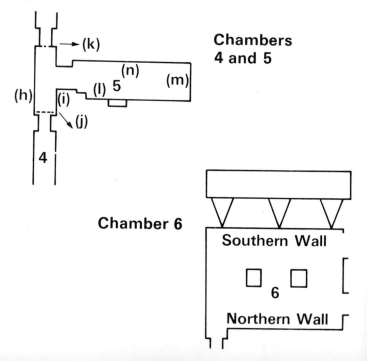

Chambers 4 and 5

Chamber 6

Southern Wall

Northern Wall

On the right-hand, northern wall, we will start above the doorway. In the fourth register (1) is a game between boatmen; they use long poles with which they attempt to thrust each other off their heavily laden vessels. Below (2) is a scene of fishing from small boats; the fishermen use weights and hooks attached to a line, and trap nets. One man, on the left, shakes fish out of a trap net into a basket. The next two registers have agricultural scenes. At (3) farmers plough the land. The plough, which is identical with the *mihrat* still used along the banks of the Nile today, is no more than a hoe enlarged by adding two long wooden arms on which the ploughman can lean to keep the furrow straight, and a pole is provided with a yoke for attaching to the draught animals. At (4) farmers use the hoe to break up the clods of earth and, to the left, rams are driven to tread the seed; the farmer in front of them feeds the leader to induce it to move forward and the farmer to the rear raises a stick. Another scatters the seed in the clods of newly broken earth, and an overseer stands with his hand on his shoulder.

Near the left-hand corner of the doorway (5) is a charming inundation scene showing cattle being driven through a canal. There is an appealing representation of a young calf being piggy-backed across the water by a herdsman. The calf turns its head back anxiously towards its mother, who raises equally anxious eyes at her offspring. The artist has suggested transparency by painting the legs of the cattle and the herdsman through the zigzag lines of the water. Representations such as these show the sensitive and nature-loving personalities of the ancient Egyptians.

Dominating this wall is a scene of Ti (6) engaged in sport amidst the teeming and colourful water-life of the papyrus groves. The parallel lines represent the papyrus stalks. Above Ti's figure are plants, birds and nests (unfortunately difficult to see). The male, female and young of a large variety of birds, each painstakingly depicted with the characteristics of the species, are shown, but are not carved to scale. Two foxes search for birds' nests. There is also a mongoose.

Ti himself watches his attendants hippo-hunting. To the right a speared hippo bellows in pain. Another has caught a crocodile in his mouth. Varieties of Nile fish are depicted in detail. To the left, on a small separate boat, a dwarf catches a fish. He holds a stick in his hand with which to club it.

All along the lower register (7) are female attendants symbolising the revenue of the nobleman's domain. Beside each is the name of the area from which the produce is brought. Note the variety of products being brought in many different baskets. All the women use one hand to hold the basket and the other is either bent to drape a small item over the lower arm, or hanging straight. The simple robes worn by the women are enhanced with necklets, bracelets and anklets. The ideal figure of a woman in the Old Kingdom was slim-waisted and small breasted. In New Kingdom reliefs women with large breasts and rounded hips were obviously admired, and by the Late Period the voluptuous woman was in vogue.

In the second register (8) there is another passage of a canal. Note how the animals are encouraged to enter the water: a calf is placed in the water and led across, and its mother, who follows, leads the rest of the cattle. A crocodile lies in wait for the calf at the other end! Further along the same register, at (9), are rare scenes showing the weaving of rush mats; bobbins are prepared and the warp placed. At (10) a dwarf and a hunchback walk their master's pet greyhounds and a monkey.

The next register (11) contains a series of charming rural scenes. From right to left: a grey cow gives birth with an expression of suffering in her eyes. She is helped by a farmer. She holds her front legs stiff with the effort. Behind her, restive calves have their hind legs bound together or are tethered to pegs in the ground. One calf is unwilling to be tied up and playfully jumps away, while the farmer, holding the rope, tries to entice it towards him with his hand. The ancient Egyptians studied the habits of various animals and accurately captured their attitudes in these murals. Great imagination is shown. For example, further to the left, a cow is being milked while its frisky calf is restrained by a herdsman; the calf turns its head towards its mother, lusting for the milk with its tongue hanging out! A farmer feeds and caresses a calf, another feeds a seated ox. Towards the end of the register (12) small furniture is being carried, and at (13) scribes are depicted with their writing equipment.

Above, at (14), fishermen draw in trawl-nets filled with catch. One fisherman shakes the fish from a long wicker-like trap into a basket, while his two neighbours, to the left, seated at a low table, cut up the fish ready for barter.

The upper registers (15) are difficult to see unless the light is good, but they show the trapping and plucking of fowl and, to the left, another scene of mat-making.

The western wall of the sacrificial chamber contains two door-shaped stelae. The slab for offerings in front of one of them is still in position. As already mentioned, this symbolic entrance was connected to the tomb chamber by means of a shaft. The scenes between the two stelae are symbolic scenes of sacrificial offerings to Ti and his family.

The southern wall, like the northern, is covered with a wide variety of activities. There are three slits in the masonry through which the statue (illuminated) in the *Serdab* can be seen.

On the extreme right (1) Ti sits before a table of *hotep*-bread; this is a stylised representation of the oldest form of bread, which was baked in a mould and then sliced. An assortment of fruit, vegetables (including beans, onions, cucumbers, leeks), fowl, meats, cakes and many varieties of wine and beer are brought by two rows of servants (2) and (3). The registers of offerings continue to the top of the wall (9), and all retain vivid colour. The central registers (10) list the offerings in hieroglyphics which denote numbers of various items in hundreds, thousands, and tens of thousands.

Immediately below Ti's feet (11) an orchestra, comprising a flautist, two harpists and two singers, is playing. The ancient Egyptians had a great sense of rhythm and love of music. Even fishermen and farmers often had a piper or singer to entertain them while they worked. The wealthy classes enjoyed music at all times of day – at their morning toilet, at meals and during leisure hours. Harps were small and usually played by a seated musician; flutes were in two sizes. The lower registers, (12) to (15), depict a variety of scenes of the slaughter of animals.

Towards the centre of the wall (16) there is a standing figure of Ti, with his wife seated beside him, touching his foot. He inspects animals brought by the peasants from his estates: gazelles and antelope, (17) to (20), and oxen, (21) and (22).

Just below Ti (23) is a Court of Justice. The scene shows three elderly peasants being forcibly brought in to make tax returns. The clerks and the scribes are represented in two rows. They squat on the ground, some writing on their raised knees, others at desks. The tax payers are villagers who have failed to pay their returns and are being brought in by officers of the law who have staves under their arms. The inscription reads: 'seizing the town rulers for a reckoning'. Such an estate office with pillared hall and scribes keeping records appeared in noblemen's tombs only in the second half of the 5th Dynasty.

Registers (24) and (25) show healthy sacrificial bulls being led by peasants; some of the bulls wear bells and fancy collars round the neck.

The lower registers on each side of the slit of the *Serdab* depict poultry (26) and cranes (27).

A large section of the extreme left-hand side of the wall has been damaged. However, the lower registers have been restored. At (28)

Ducks in relief. (Tomb of Ti)

Farmers lead cranes. (Tomb of Ti)

men blow into a furnace with tubes to heat a crucible of copper. Below (29) sculptors and stone-workers make statues, and (30) carpenters are at work; they make a door, a chest, and a bed with a headrest beneath it. Note the carpenters sawing planks, using the bow-drill for a cylinder seal, slitting a board with a copper tool, hammering with a mallet and polishing the bedstead.

In the lower register (31) there are leather-workers, and an interesting scene of bartering: a leather pouch is exchanged for a pair of sandals, an animal skin for two pots of oil and (to the extreme right) two men are exchanging sticks; one leans backwards as though unwilling to go through with the deal while his companion leans enthusiastically forward with an encouraging smile.

On each side of the *Serdab* men are depicted burning incense. The original statue in the *Serdab*, now in Cairo Museum, was one of the few found intact. In its place stands a cast. Several other statues of Ti were broken.

The eastern wall is divided into two sections, with Ti and his wife at the centre. Behind them, on the right-hand side of the wall, there are three shipbuilding scenes which are particularly well

Trading sticks. (Tomb of Ti)

preserved. They show the entire operation, from the selection of suitable tree trunks for the hull, through all stages of shaping, assembling and finishing the vessel. Workmen, using hammers, chisels, drills, saws and axes can be seen milling over the hull. Shipbuilding was an active industry from very early times, when seaworthy ships sailed across the Mediterranean to Byblos to bring back cedarwood. One of the oldest texts relating to journeys across the Mediterranean dates to the reign of Sneferu, who recorded that forty vessels sailed to Byblos in a single year.

On the left-hand side of the wall Ti inspects harvest operations, which are represented in seven scenes. Registers (1) and (2) show the wheat being reaped; at (2) the second and third figures from the left are a flautist and a singer who accompany the operation. Register (3) depicts a series of activities including the tying up of the wheat into bundles and loading them onto donkeys. To the right a group of donkey-drivers play a game with sticks as they wait. Register (4) shows the donkeys being held as the loads are placed

EASTERN WALL OF TOMB OF TI

Hunting and boat-building. (Tomb of Ptah-hotep)

on their backs to be borne to the granary. Note that the donkey to the right, carrying the grain sheaths towards Ti, has its foal in front of it. Register (5) shows the ears of wheat being taken from the sacks and piled into heaps. Register (6) shows oxen and donkeys treading the grain, which is then piled in great heaps by means of three-pronged forks (7). On the bottom row, to the right, women winnow the grain with small boards to separate the grain from the chaff and, to the right, other women place the grain in sacks.

As we leave the chamber, another glance above the doorway will reveal the already described beginning of the harvest operations: tilling the land, ploughing and sowing.

It should be noted that there are no representations of a funerary nature on the walls of the tombs of the 5th Dynasty. There is not a single deity being placated with offerings. So strong was the conviction that life after death was a mere continuation of the good life on earth, that no pandering to deities was considered necessary, and no prayers for guidance were needed.

If these bold and beautiful creations on the walls of the tombs of Sakkara mirror the soul of ancient Egypt, then we can see that here were a people who conscientiously channelled their energies in the services of the living, and who had a wholesome view of life and of the world around them.

TOMB OF PTAH-HOTEP (Inspector of Priests)
Ptah-hotep was one of the highest officials in the land in the reign of Djedkare (*c.* 2380 B.C.). The reliefs in this tomb are among the highest achievements of Old Kingdom art, and they are in an excellent state of preservation. Though the tomb is smaller than that of Ti, the plan is more developed. The entrance, to the north, leads to a corridor (1), a pillared hall (2), a small antechamber (3) and the sacrificial chamber (4). The chamber to the west of the pillared hall (5) was dedicated to Akhet-hotep, a son of Ptah-hotep. In the rectangular chamber (6) is an anonymous mutilated mummy in a stone sarcophagus.

Description
The corridor (1) contains unfinished reliefs, enabling us to see the various stages of mural decoration. To the left (a) the red line drawings of the original design can be seen on the prepared stone surface, along with corrections by the master-artist in black. To the right (b) there are various stages of low relief sculpture: the first

stage involved the carving away of the background; this may not have been too difficult a task on soft newly-quarried limestone. However, to ensure an even surface was not so simple. The next stage was to work rough detail on the projecting figures. Full detail of clothing, hair and physical features were then worked on. Then final touches were added. In the lower registers, servants carry fowl in their arms. Note the number of different ways in which they carry them. They bear them towards Ptah-hotep, who stands near the end of the right-hand wall (c). This is an excellent figure of the

TOMB OF PTAH-HOTEP

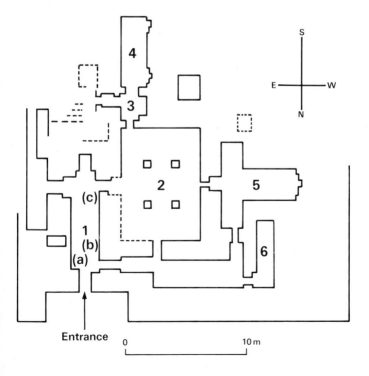

Entrance

0   10 m

owner of the tomb. It has sometimes been said that the ancient Egyptians showed great understanding of animals and birds, and were able to represent them in motion, whereas man was the least competently depicted. However, the fine detail of the muscles on Ptah-hotep's arm, around his belly, on his knee-cap and calf, clearly indicate a sound knowledge of anatomy. Though the squared shoulders with head and limbs in profile may seem somewhat strange to us, the artist was nevertheless portraying the most characteristic features of the human body. It was considered that the side of the face was able to give greater detail of its contour than the full face, while, on the other hand, the front view of the eye disclosed greater detail than the side view. It is true that the ponderous and measured walk of an ox, the waddle of geese, and the grace of the antelope were captured with great sensitivity. But so, too, were the healthy, energetic stance of the important official, the heavily built and well-fed supervisors of workmen, and the shorter, sturdier figures of farmers and labourers, accurately depicted.

The square hall (2), the roof of which is supported by four pillars, is undecorated and was never completed. However, it provides an excellent example of the use of slits in the masonry to illuminate windowless chambers. These are situated in the roof and also at points where the wall meets the roof. The slit is angled to enable the light to filter into the chamber, with no dazzling beams of direct sunlight.

The antechamber (3) leads to the sacrificial chamber (4), the most perfectly preserved of this period and retaining much of the original colouring. The right-hand wall (d) has two door-shaped stelae, representing the symbolic entrance to the tomb. The right-

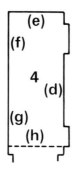

hand stele is elaborately decorated, in the palace-façade fashion. It is painted to imitate reed matting. Between the stelae is a representation of Ptah-hotep, dressed in the panther-skin of a High Priest, seated at a richly furnished table of offerings, raising a goblet to his lips. Note the varieties of poultry, meats, breads and cakes, vegetables, and fruit, carved to fill the space in a most aesthetic manner. The interrelation of the various items gives a tapestry effect. In the upper row priests make offerings, and in the lower three rows, servants bear gifts. On the rear wall (e), Ptah-hotep is represented once again seated before a table of offerings. Immediately in front of him is the traditional stylised *hotep*-bread, on a table. Beside the table are copper basins and ewers in order that he may cleanse himself before partaking of the food. In the upper row, women representing various farming areas bear him the produce of his estates, with the area and the product detailed in hieroglyphics beside each figure. In the second row animals are being thrown and slaughtered, and in the two lower registers more offering-bearers are depicted.

The eastern wall provides a comprehensive catalogue of events in the life of the deceased. There are two themes, each in seven registers. On the right-hand side of the wall (f) Ptah-hotep inspects 'gifts and tributes brought from his estates of the North and of the South'. From the top register we see a scene of wrestling youths, and seven boys running. Note that the front boy has his arm tied. The second and third rows show men dragging cages containing lions, a frame with gazelles bound together in groups, and other cages containing hares and hedgehogs. To the left of the caged animals, the nobleman's greyhounds are being taken for a walk on leashes. The fourth row, unfortunately damaged, depicts herdsmen and cattle. A cow can be seen giving birth with the aid of a peasant who gently guides the calf into the world. A number of other calves struggle to disengage themselves from the cords that bind them to plants. The fifth and sixth rows depict cattle being brought to Ptah-hotep for inspection. A lame herdsman leads a magnificent bull with an adornment around its neck. In the bottom register are domestic poultry; if the texts are to be believed, then we know that Ptah-hotep possessed '121,000 geese of one variety, 11,210 of another variety, 120,000 small geese, 111,200 goslings and 1,225 swans'.

On the left-hand side of the wall (g), Ptah-hotep 'witnesses all the pleasant activities that take place in the whole country.' These include, in the top row, youths wrestling, and bare-legged men plucking papyrus reeds in the marshes; these are tied into bundles and carried away on their backs.

The second row shows a series of games being played: four girls play a swing-around game with arms extended, boys play 'touch' with one boy kneeling in the centre, and the game on the right is still played in Lower Nubia today; it involves two boys seated, facing each other, with arms and feet extended towards each other, while their colleagues vault over them. The game is now known as 'Khaza la wizza'.

In the third row viticulture is represented: grapes are being picked from vines on trellises (note a gardener watering them) and they are either trodden with the feet or crushed in sacks between sticks.

The fourth row shows animal life: a hound seizing an antelope, a lion devouring an ox, and animals mating. Towards the centre of the wall a mongoose can be seen, and a delightful representation of a hedgehog emerging from its hole with a cricket in its mouth.

The fifth row shows a kneeling hunter pointing out an ill-fated cow to his two hounds. The cow has been tied up as bait and as the lion seizes its muzzle in its jaws, while fastening its claws into the animal's neck, the terrified cow releases its bowels.

The sixth row depicts men working in the marshes. They fish, weave nets and make papyrus boats. Note the group of men in the centre netting birds: they hold the trap net firmly from their seated position, and then on a signal from the foreman, make a sudden backward movement to draw it tight; some of the birds escape, but the captured specimens are placed in boxes and borne away. The fisherman on the extreme left is scaling his catch with a knife.

In the seventh, the bottom row, is a scene in which the artist seems to have given free rein to his imagination. Boatmen lash out at one another in somewhat wild abandon with their long poles from their heavily laden papyrus skiffs. This scene is sometimes described as boatmen's quarrels. However, the text makes it clear that this was a game, as the inscription tells of cries of encouragement from spectators. To the extreme left an obese overseer is seated in a boat receiving a drink from a boatman.

When viewing the northern wall (h), above the doorway, one should recall that this is a 5th Dynasty tomb, and the life depicted was being enjoyed at a time when Europe, America and most of western Asia were still in the Stone Age. The highly sophisticated scene then takes on added meaning. This part of the wall is somewhat faded, but Ptah-hotep can nevertheless be seen, on the right, seated at his morning toilet with his greyhounds beneath his chair and a pet monkey held by his valet. Manicurists work on his hands, pedicurists on his feet, while musicians entertain him (in two rows to the right). These include harpers, flute players, a singer cupping his hand round his ear, and a conductor beating time with his hands. Above the musicians is a row of dwarfs stringing beads. Below the musicians are two rows of officials, seated on the ground, awaiting their daily instructions. To the left of the doorway are offerings and slaughter scenes.

Retracing our steps to the pillared hall (2), we enter chamber (5), which was dedicated to Ptah-hotep's son. The reliefs are not as fine as those of the sacrificial chamber. They are the usual offering scenes and representations of storehouses. Note the varieties of pottery. Facing, at (i) is a stele. There is, however, a particularly well-preserved representation to the right, at (j). It shows the figure of Ptah-hotep's son, Akhet-hotep, also called Ptah-hotep, in the act of writing on a large slate with a long reed pen.

The tomb of Ptah-hotep proved to be extremely valuable in the deciphering of hieroglyphics, in view of the determinative symbols beside the clearly sculpted words.

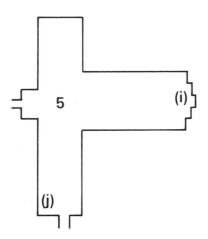

124

Cow lusts after its own milk. (Tomb of Kagemni)

TOMB OF NEFER (open by special permission)
This charming tomb of the Director of the Chorus and Inspector of the Court was discovered in 1964 beneath the great causeway of the pyramid of Unas by Ahmed Moussa, then Inspector of Antiquities. Apart from the quality and detail of the wall reliefs, the tomb contains a wooden coffin at the foot of a shaft on the eastern wall with the oldest known intact mummy, which is over 4,300 years old. It is the body of a singer called Wati, who could not afford a tomb of his own and was buried in the family vault of Nefer, whose sons he knew. Although mummification had not been perfected in the 5th Dynasty, the body was found in nearly perfect condition, and was so carefully wrapped that even the contours of fingernails and a callous on the foot were preserved in linen. A thin layer of light green plaster had been modelled over the whole body, with details of eyebrows and moustache, set in relief, and the nipples were painted on the chest.

On the right-hand wall on entering are six registers, depicting vessels (1st register), milking of a cow (2nd register), mating and the birth of a calf (3rd register), the preparation of meat and liquid refreshment in the outhouses of a kitchen (4th register), and (5th register) manuring fields and scenes of cattle.

The deceased and his family are represented on the right-hand wall with a unique representation showing Nefer's wife, seated with a child, beneath a pergola, watching dancers.

On the rear wall the reliefs are faint, but there is another unique scene (5th register from the bottom) showing the planting of onions, lettuce and other garden vegetables in two vegetable beds. There is also a fine representation of the gathering of papyrus which, as the bound roots show, is being transported for transplantation. Above this scene, to the right, note the large tree laden with fruit, and the squatting figures collecting the sycamore-figs.

On the left-hand wall there are some more unusual scenes, including a grape harvest with a tame baboon giving assistance, and a man getting a flogging from his master.

A ladder leads to a pit in the floor. In the tomb chamber the mummy of Wati lies naked, apart from the beaded necklace around his neck and a false beard of stiffened linen. When found the mummy held a long cane in one hand and a sceptre in the other.

TOMB OF NIANKH-KHNUM AND KHNUM-HOTEP (open by special permission)
This double tomb was discovered in 1965. The co-owners stand face

to face near each other, and it was at first thought that they were brothers. In fact they had different parents, and the only thing that links them together appears to be friendship, established over a long period of sharing the same profession. Both Niankh-Khnum and Khnum-Hotep were Priests of the Sun Temple of Nyuserre and Manicurists of the Court. The scenes of bird-hunting, stock-rearing etc. are repeated in each half of the tomb.

PYRAMID OF UNAS
General
Unas raised his pyramid near the south-west corner of the Step Pyramid complex. Some of the blocks used in its construction were taken from Zoser's monument, constructed nearly three centuries earlier, indicating that, even then, it was falling in ruin. This small pyramid of the last of the pharaohs of the 5th Dynasty forms the prototype for all the pyramids of the 6th Dynasty.

The original height of Unas' pyramid was only about eighteen and a half metres and, like the earlier 5th Dynasty pyramids at Abu Sir, it had a core of loose blocks and rubble, and the facing only was of hewn limestone. On the southern face is an inscription by Khaemwas, son of Ramses II, who, in identifying the owner of this and many other pyramids, may be regarded as the first Egyptologist. When the pyramid was first opened by Maspero in 1881, the tomb chamber was found to contain an obsidian sarcophagus standing close to the western wall. The cover had been dragged off, but the remains of a mummy were found inside. Fragments of a skull, a shin bone, and an arm were also found in the tomb chamber.

The Pyramid Texts
The Pyramid of Unas is of immense historical importance. Up to this point in history the pyramids were unadorned. On the walls of the central and tomb chambers of Unas' pyramid, however, and also on those of four of his successors of the 6th Dynasty, texts were written. These are long columns of inscribed hieroglyphs known as the Pyramid Texts. They are the earliest and the least corrupt of the mortuary literature of ancient Egypt.

The Pyramid Texts contain some 714 'utterances'. Some are modified versions of hymns and rituals that preceded and accompanied the interment of the body; others are prayers for the release of the soul, or *Ba*, from the body; and a large section of the texts itemises offerings of food, drink and clothing for use in the afterlife.

Pyramid of Unas. (5th Dynasty)

Cartouche of the Pharaoh Unas, from his Mortuary Temple.

They are believed to stem from very early oral traditions, or from earlier texts either perished or undiscovered. Some of the utterances of speeches include the phrase 'Cast the sand from thy face', for example, which must date to the pre-dynastic burial practices when the body was placed in a simple grave, wrapped in cloth or animal skin. Descriptions of the mythological battles between Horus and Set, on the other hand, as chief deities of Upper and Lower Egypt, reflected the national discord during the first two dynasties.

Though these texts have been preserved in tombs, and their purpose was funerary, the priests who ordered their inscription had long preached their content. Each utterance is preceded with the phrase 'Recite the Words', clearly indicating that they were current ritual.

Some of the pyramids contain identical texts, but few are repeated in all the pyramids. Some of the later pyramids reveal passages not included in earlier ones. It would appear, therefore, that the oral traditions were so extensive that selections could be made of those passages which suited the individual taste. Even at this early stage, therefore, there is evidence of choice, just as with the mural decorations in the tombs of the noblemen.

Some of the hieroglyphic symbols included the images of dangerous living creatures such as the scorpion. To render such potentially hostile creatures impotent, the sculptors of the texts sometimes carved them in separate halves or, in the case of the scorpion, deprived it of its tail.

After the fall of the Old Kingdom, the provincial lords appropriated the royal funerary texts and inscribed them on their coffins. At first these Coffin Texts were inscribed on the four inner surfaces of the coffin only, the outside being reserved for the name and titles of the deceased, along with a short prayer, and naturally some selection was made. Rituals referring specifically to the God-king were either eliminated or recomposed to make them appropriate for rankless individuals.

Gradually more verses and rituals were included in the Coffin Texts, and when they became too numerous for the available space, both inside and outside the coffin, they began to be written on papyrus, which could be rolled up and placed near the mummified body. The priests and their wives copied the texts, and in their hands it slowly became standardised.

By the Middle Kingdom, the Court of Justice, where Osiris was enthroned with his judges of the dead in the underworld, began clearly to develop, and the mortuary texts began to form into distinct chapters or sections covering specific rituals with clearly defined limits. A notable addition was a set of apprehensions of the hazards of the after-life. The priests began to tint the underworld with danger. They invented a land of darkness and terror, with cascades of boiling water and dragon-like creatures which could rob the deceased of his mortuary food and drink. But they also prescribed potent charms to protect the deceased from the dangers at each stage of the journey through the region of the underworld. They gave him, moreover, a choice of Two Ways: a map of the journey inscribed in the coffin.

Just as the Coffin Texts of the Middle Kingdom were drawn from the Pyramid Texts of the Old Kingdom, the former formed the nucleus of the mortuary texts of the New Kingdom. These are the Chapters of Going Forth by Day, popularly known as the Book of the Dead. The term is, of course, misleading, for no such book ever existed. The New Kingdom version of the texts, commonly written on papyri, was the end product of twelve centuries of accumulated, revised and modified rituals, prayers, ceremonies and traditions. By this time, however, they had reached their final, unified and modified form. They were clearly divided into sections and embellished with vignettes. The selections varied according to the size of the papyrus roll (often prepared in advance by the priests and their assistants), or to the taste of the purchaser.

The priests also developed and popularised a number of the funerary texts of the Middle Kingdom, including the Book of him who is in the Underworld, and the Book of the Gates, describing the journey of the sun through the subterranean region during the twelve hours of night. If the deceased deviated from one of the two paths and went astray, there was a charm to save him from entering 'the place of execution of the Gods', a charm to prevent him from being overpowered by the forces of evil, a charm to prevent him from walking with his head downwards, and a magic verse to quieten his heart in the awesome presence of Osiris in the underworld. The priests accentuated the dangers in order to sell hope for redemption, and they grew steadily richer.

Naturally the Book of the Dead bears little resemblance to the Pyramid Texts, apart from certain prayers and rituals accompanying the burial and to obtain the release of the soul.

Description
The entrance is at the centre of the northern façade, on ground

level but beneath the lowest course of stone. An inclined passage, 1·40 metres high, leads directly to an antechamber (1), followed by a straight corridor where there are three enormous slabs of granite to block the tomb (2), leading to a central, nearly square chamber (3). To the left (4) is a small room which has a flat roof and three recesses, devoid of ornament. To the right (5) is the rectangular tomb chamber containing the undecorated sarcophagus and its lid. Both the central chamber and the tomb chamber have pointed roofs; the upper edges of the large limestone blocks lean against one another, while the lower edges rest on a ledge running round the chamber. The first row of slabs is surmounted by a second, the second by a third, and the three together hold the burial chamber safe from the excessive thrust of the superstructure.

The Pyramid Texts are carved in fine detail into the stone and filled with blue pigment. They cover all the available wall space, apart from the walls behind and beside the sarcophagus, which are painted to represent the façade of a building.

The pharaoh's name, Unas, can be seen carved in oblong cartouches on all the walls. The texts declare that Unas did not depart

PYRAMID OF UNAS

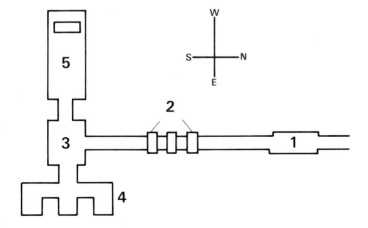

dead. Unas departed living. Unas did not die. Unas rose up. Unas stood up. Unas overcame death. And since Unas overcame death, as Osiris overcame death, he became, in death, Osiris himself.

The texts call Unas to: 'Rise and live again, as Osiris lives; for Ra (the Sun-god) receives you (the deceased pharaoh), soul (*Ba*) in heaven, body (*Khat*) in earth.'

There are also long series of descriptions recounting the efforts of Horus in the resurrection of the pharaoh (as Osiris). Horus collects Unas' limbs. Horus gave Unas his Eye (symbol of devotion). Horus avenged Unas' death. There is no more mighty god than the risen pharaoh because his son, Horus, made him so.

Causeway

A small section of the one-kilometre-long causeway linking the mortuary and valley temples has been reconstructed. Wherever possible, fragments of the relief were used. Some of the scenes show successions of offerings from the royal estate; others show groups of wild animals fleeing from hounds and hunters. There is a scene of columns being transported from Elephantine, and a particularly interesting representation of the Egyptian fleet returning from the Phoenician coast with Semitic Syrians, recognisable by their characteristic features and distinctive hair style. The famous 'famine reliefs' in the Louvre and in the Cairo Museum came from this causeway.

Note should be taken of the manner in which the roof of the reconstructed section of the causeway was designed, with a slit in the centre, so slanted that the sunlight could shine on to the inscribed walls. This manner of illuminating the reliefs also provided an outlet for the rising heat, and even in mid-summer it provided a cool, shady processional avenue.

Two huge dummy boats were excavated from boat-pits beside the causeway. They had been covered with limestone blocks in the shape of a hull. (See Work in Progress pages 174 and 175.)

1 33

Section of covered causeway linking the mortuary and valley temples of Pyramid of Unas.

CHAPTER 5   6th DYNASTY
(2345–2181 B.C.)

PYRAMIDS

All the pharaohs of the 6th Dynasty constructed their pyramids at Sakkara on the same plan as that of Unas. They have all collapsed into shapeless mounds of rubble. Like the Pyramid of Unas, the two inner chambers were decorated with Pyramid Texts.

PYRAMID OF TETI (open on request)
This was first opened in 1881. It was called the 'prison pyramid' by local inhabitants, from a local tradition that near its ruins was the prison where Joseph the Patriarch was confined. It is in a very bad state of repair, its outer facing having been used as a quarry in ancient times. The wooden sarcophagus found in the tomb chamber is now in Cairo Museum. To the east are ruins of a mortuary temple.

PYRAMID OF PEPI I
The Pyramid of Pepi I which gave Memphis its name (p. 29) is situated in south Sakkara.

Like that of Teti it is very dilapidated, now measuring only some 12 metres in height. The whole of the centre has fallen away and the different layers of limestone blocks, leaning against one another to hold the burial chamber safe from the excessive thrust of the superstructure, can be seen. Robbers originally forced an entrance, and the black basalt sarcophagus was completely wrecked in an effort to get at the mummy. Cartouches of the pharaoh in the Pyramid Texts were cut out. Overlooked in the burial chamber, however, was a granite Canopic chest containing alabaster Canopic jars, which are now in Cairo Museum (see Work in Progress, p. 176).

PYRAMID OF MERENRE
This was known by the Arabs as *Haram-as-Sayyadin*, or the 'Pyramid of the Hunters'. It was never finished, and was, moreover,

destroyed by tomb robbers who broke into it and wrecked the walls of the inner chambers. The black basalt sarcophagus, which was opened by the robbers, is in good condition. A mummy, now in Cairo Museum, was found inside it, stripped of everything valuable but in a fair stage of preservation. The method of mummification indicates that it may be the body of a pharaoh of a later period. The square granite container for the Canopic jars was found empty (see Work in Progress, p. 176).

PYRAMID OF PEPI II
Pepi II came to the throne as a child of six. Manetho's statement that he died a centenarian is now doubted by modern Egyptologists. His pyramid closely resembles that of his brother and predecessor Merenre.

The 3rd Dynasty Step Pyramid survived while the 6th Dynasty Pyramids fell into ruin.

PYRAMID OF PEPI II's QUEEN UDJEBETEN

This small, poorly built pyramid was constructed with the mortuary temple to the east, but with its doors to the north, facing the direction of the Queen's husband's pyramid. The tomb chamber is decorated with some utterances from the Pyramid Texts. This is the first instance of such inscriptions on a tomb other than that of a pharaoh.

MASTABAS
General

The absence of royal monuments after the reign of Pepi II shows the complete impoverishment of the royal house; naturally there was a corresponding loss of prestige for the God-king. The provincial aristocracy attempted to bring their provinces into greater prominence; they vied for power and began to agitate for independence.

With the restructuring of society human values changed. When the God-king ceased to be the symbol of strength and the authority of the state, the people, who could not conceive of order except in terms of leadership or kingship, turned to Osiris as the symbol of dead kingship and rebirth.

During the 6th Dynasty the mastabas of the noblemen indicated that they no longer regarded the afterlife as a mere continuation of a happy earthly experience; they began to inscribe prayers in their tombs, and the façades began to bear such inscriptions as: 'Osiris, Lord of Busiris, Lord of the West, shall favour them,' '. . . a boon which Osiris, Lord of Busiris, gives . . .' or 'One revered by Osiris.' There are also, in some instances, prayers addressed to Anubis, the God of Embalming, to grant safe entry to the hereafter.

TOMB OF MERERUKA

This tomb belongs to the son-in-law of the Pharaoh Teti, and is situated immediately north-west of the tomb of his pharaoh. It was discovered in 1893 by M. J. de Morgan, and has now been restored. It is a large complex comprising thirty-three chambers and corridors; the largest group (A) is devoted to Mereruka himself, an important official as well as a priest; smaller groups were devoted to his son, Meri-Teti (B) and his wife Hert-watet-khet (C). All the stelae in this tomb, for Mereruka, his son, and his wife, face the west, which was regarded as the entrance to the underworld. The stelae in the 5th Dynasty tombs face east, towards the rising sun.

TOMB OF MERERUKA

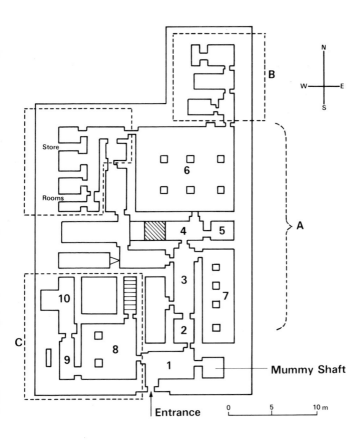

Store Rooms

6

B

4 5

A

3 7

2

10

C

9 8

1 Mummy Shaft

Entrance

N
W   E
S

0   5   10 m

138

The reliefs of this tomb are badly damaged, and are not of such fine quality as those of the 5th Dynasty. However, the highly diversified murals, including some representations not elsewhere found, make this one of the most important tombs on the Sakkara plateau.

To the right of the entrance (a) is a representation of Mereruka seated as an artist, depicted painting three deities representing the three seasons of the agricultural year. The *Akhet,* or inundation, which began on July 19; the *Perit,* 'going out', or season for ploughing and sowing, which began on November 15; and the *Shemu,* or harvest, which began on March 16. He sits before an easel with his writing apparatus hanging from his shoulder, holding a shell containing colour in one hand, and a brush in the other.

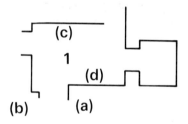

To the left of the entrance (b) is a representation of Mereruka and Meri-Teti (the boy has the side-lock of youth) holding a lotus stalk in one hand and a hoopoe bird in the other. Behind them are Mereruka's wife and several rows of attendants.

In the first chamber (1), the upper rear wall (c) has been destroyed, but in the lower areas Mereruka's legs can be seen as he stands in a skiff from which he is spearing two fishes with a two-pronged spear. From the two smaller boats men are securing hippo by means of snares and poles. Note two grasshoppers and a small frog among the aquatic plants.

On the opposite wall (d) is an exceptional marsh scene. Mereruka hunts from a boat. Birds, fish and hippo (one with a crocodile in its mouth) are depicted in the reed-filled waters. The ancient Egyptians had a great love of outdoor sport, and swamp and marsh scenes such as these are depicted in naturalistic detail.

In chamber (2), on the right-hand wall (e), Mereruka and his wife (to the left) inspect various industrial activities on the estate. These are represented in six rows. On the bottom rows are jewellers, some of whom are dwarfs, soldering, hammering, casting and fitting together the exquisite jewellery which is displayed in the row above them. Above this, to the left, the chief goldsmith weighs the precious metal, and scribes record the quantity before it is delivered to the craftsmen. To the right, metal workers are depicted, along with their products. Above, in the third row, statues in the likeness of the nobleman himself are being towed towards the tomb. In the fourth row, carpenters are at work making bedsteads. The two top rows show stone-workers fashioning a variety of vessels.

On the opposite wall (f), Mereruka and his wife are depicted in a spirited hunting scene in the desert, with hounds, lion, hares, and oxen depicted.

In chamber (3), on the right-hand wall (g), to the right, Mereruka and his wife and attendants watch fish-catching. Note the variety

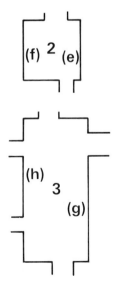

of methods used: the trap-net, wicker-baskets, and the draw-net. Further along the same wall Mereruka and his wife go to market preceded by their servants, one of whom leads pet animals on a leash.

On the left-hand wall (h), is a representation of the estate headquarters. This is a delightful scene showing clerks seated in a hall with lotus-bud columns, while the village elders are being forcibly dragged to give evidence on their faulty tax returns. One man has been stripped, and his arms and feet are bound round a post where he is being beaten. Tax payments were made in produce: grain, livestock, wine, honey, cloth, and so on. The crops were stored in granaries and storehouses which formed the government treasury. Further along the wall Mereruka and his wife inspect the offering of sacrifices to statues of the deceased.

Only a few reliefs have been preserved in Chamber (4), which contains a stele and a *Serdab*. Chamber (5) contains a number of scenes on the left-hand wall (i) of the deceased receiving produce from the estates. In the lower row grapes are being trodden and pressed into containers. There is also a row of ten barns or storehouses.

Chamber (6) is the sacrificial chamber, containing six square pillars on which Mereruka is depicted on each face. Near the centre of the chamber is a stone ring for tethering the sacrificial animal. In the recess, facing us as we enter the chamber, a statue of Mereruka, in the vigour of manhood, strides forward with his shoulders thrown back and his head erect. His lips smile and the statue seems to step forward from the darkness of the tomb chamber where the *Khat* lies embalmed, to cross the threshold to the afterlife. On the days of offerings, the family of the deceased would come to this chamber, and this huge painted figure would seem, in his 'advancing' posture, to be imbued with life. Since Graeco-Roman times

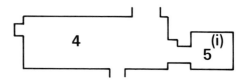

Mereruka's statue has been protected by the flagged paving linking the Apis Temples, which passed exactly overhead.

Moving anti-clockwise round this chamber we come first to harvest operations (j) including the reaping and winnowing of corn.

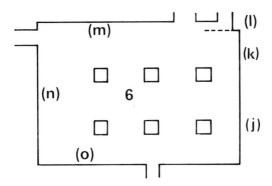

Fishermen haul in the catch. (Tomb of Mereruka)

Further along the wall (k) is a scene of Mereruka and his wife, seated before a table playing a game that looks something like chess. Above the doorway, to the right of the statue (l), are representations of various games being played by boys and girls. These include a tug-of-war, a 'swing around', and touching a crouching player with the foot while attempting to evade his hands. The girls exchange copper mirrors in a game of forfeit.

The reliefs to the left of the statue (m) show Mereruka inspecting domestic animals (in the lower four rows), including gazelles, goats, antelope and cattle; also the forced feeding of a tame hyaena. Note the old man conducted by his two sons; and Mereruka seated in a carrying-chair with a large retinue including two dwarfs leading dogs.

On the western wall, at (n), the scenes are somewhat damaged. They depict large seaworthy vessels being made ready for sail across the Mediterranean to Byblos. The movements of the figures of the sailors and the variety of their poses are less conventional and stylised than in the agricultural scenes.

On the southern wall (o), only the bottom section has been preserved. This shows a funeral procession, which is rare, with priests and dancers; the men bear a large chest and funerary equipment.

We will now retrace our steps to chamber (3) and enter chamber (7) to the east. This chamber is supported by four pillars, each bearing incised reliefs of the deceased. Travelling anti-clockwise, we see Mereruka seated in an easy chair (p) receiving various gifts in boxes and vessels. Further along the wall, at (q), there is an

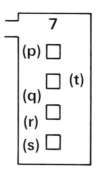

intimate and delightful scene depicting Mereruka and his wife seated together on a large couch; she plays the harp to her husband, who holds a fly whisk, and he is obviously attentive to her music. At (r) Mereruka and his wife stand, hand in hand, watching their servants preparing their bed (s), which stands beneath a canopy.

On the opposite wall there are various scenes of the deceased and his wife, with attendants, being brought gifts and offerings. Towards the centre of the wall (t) are two rows of male and female dancers performing a variety of movements. Though the quality of the reliefs in this chamber is poor, the scenes, especially those of domesticity, are unusual.

Retracing our steps to the entrance of the tomb we now enter the chambers to the west. These were constructed for Mereruka's wife, and hers is the predominant figure. The first chamber (8) has two square columns. Mereruka's wife was a princess, and on the walls to the right and left she is depicted receiving various gifts from her attendants. On the wall behind the columns (u) she is depicted with her son and daughter. Four servants bear her on an enormous carrying-chair adorned with lions. There is also a fishing scene; and another of the capture of wild bulls.

Chamber (9) has scenes of Mereruka's wife watching dancing.

The main feature of Chamber (10) is an elaborate stele with a square block in front of it which once bore a sacrificial tablet. Each of the side walls (v) and (w), is decorated with reliefs of the

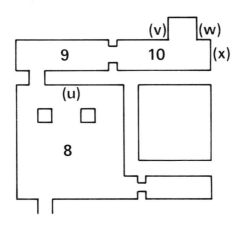

TOMB OF KAGEMNI

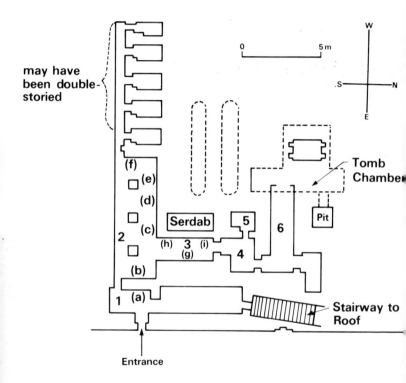

may have been double-storied

W
S — N
E

0 ____ 5 m

(f)
(e)
(d)
(c)
2
(h) 3 (i)
(g)
(b)
1 (a)

Serdab 5 6

4

Tomb Chamber

Pit

Stairway to Roof

Entrance

deceased seated at a table while servants bear her flowers, food and refreshments. Note the light colour of her skin.

On the short wall (x), she is depicted, with her son, in a huge carrying-chair decorated with a lion. Near her are three dogs and a pet ape.

Abutting the tomb of Mereruka and against the wall of the tomb of Kagemni (see rear end paper) are a series of chapels dating to the Middle Kingdom. They are worth noting for two reasons: first, because there are few **Middle Kingdom** monuments on the Sakkara plateau; second, because the Chapel of Ihy, an important official in the reign of the 12th Dynasty pharaoh Amenemhet 1, contains scenes which are identical with those of the neighbouring shrine of Thethu of the 6th Dynasty. It would seem that Ihy instructed his artists to copy the earlier reliefs.

Beyond the Middle Kingdom chapels is the **Street of 6th Dynasty Tombs** discovered and cleared by Loret in 1899. The most well-preserved are:

TOMB OF KAGEMNI
This tomb, situated immediately to the right of Mereruka's, belongs to the Vizier, who was also High Priest and Judge. He seems to have been honoured after his death, as many personal names were formed with his as an element. The tomb is a large tomb and some of the reliefs are of excellent quality. The tomb has two unusual features: one is a stairway to the right of the entrance antechamber (1), leading to the roof; the other is the two large chambers, some ten and a half metres in length, which were probably made to house funerary barges.

Fishing from papyrus boats. (Tomb of Kagemni)

146

TOMB OF ANKH-MAHOR

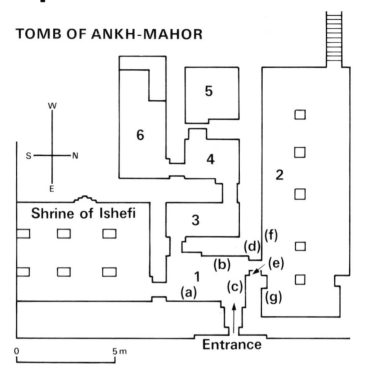

On the wall facing the entrance (a) is a scene of fishing with trap nets. The door to the left-hand rear wall leads to the pillared hall (2). Moving anti-clockwise, we come first to a scene of dancers, women clapping, and acrobats (b) near the bottom of the wall. At (c) is a scene of fishing with a multi-hooked rod, and hippo-spearing (this is in good condition). The deceased and his attendants are in canoes (the upper part of the wall is damaged). At (d) are representations of the lassoing of a cow, and of a small fat puppy with a pig-like face, being fed. Cattle ford an inundated river (e), and on the rear wall (f) a mother on a boat feeds her baby—an unusual representation.

Chamber (3) leads off the pillared hall to the north. The reliefs include fishing scenes at (g), with fishermen returning with their catch in baskets and, at (h), fowling scenes. Note the birds in the trees, and the leaves on the trees. At (i) is a scene showing the feeding of animals and birds, as well as scribes registering their number to the nobleman on the extreme right.

Above the doorway leading to chamber (4), a dwarf looks after the nobleman's pets. He is seated in a somewhat cramped position in a carrying-chair. Chamber (4) contains offering scenes. Chamber (5) has a shaft. Chamber (6), a long narrow chamber, contains a well-preserved stele at the far end. This chamber, too, contains scenes of offerings.

TOMB OF ANKH-MAHOR (known as the 'Physician's Tomb')

This is known as the Physician's Tomb in view of the remarkable representations of surgical operations.

In the first chamber (1), moving clockwise, we see various cattle scenes at (a), agricultural scenes at (b), and at (c) is a representation of a dog with a curly pig-like tail and snout, somewhat like the fat puppy being fed in the tomb of Kagemni.

The surgical operations are in the doorway leading to the pillared hall. To the left (d) is an operation on a man's toe. To the right (e) is the circumcision of a youth. The text explains the proceedings. In one line of hieroglyphics the physician assures the youth that 'I shall not do wrong to you.' In the next line the patient is encouraged: 'Hold yourself firm and do not give way,' to which the youth responds: 'I shall do to please you.' Bodies of Egyptians from predynastic burial grounds (*c.* 4000 B.C.) were found to be circumcised.

In the pillared hall (2) is a particularly noteworthy scene (which is not in very good condition). At (f) we see scenes of mourning: grief is rendered in heart-rending detail. Men and women, wailing and moaning, fainting or seeking support in their sorrow, are depicted in the upper register. Such funeral processions only began to be represented in tombs towards the end of the 5th and during the 6th Dynasties, which may indicate that some of the inherent optimism of the people of the Nile valley, and their conviction of a happy afterlife, were wavering.

On the other side of the doorway (g) are scenes of dancing (also in poor condition).

Chambers 3–6 are sealed.

TOMB OF NEFER SHESHEM-PTAH (known as Sheshi)

This is a badly damaged tomb and is usually closed to the public. It belongs to the Steward of the Pyramid of Teti and contains some unusual scenes in chamber (3). There is a door-shaped stele with complete figures of the deceased emerging on either side. Above the stele is a recess with a bust of the deceased which looks into the shrine from the window above the lintel. This idea of a bust peeping into a shrine is unusual, and rather curious.

TOMB OF IDOUT

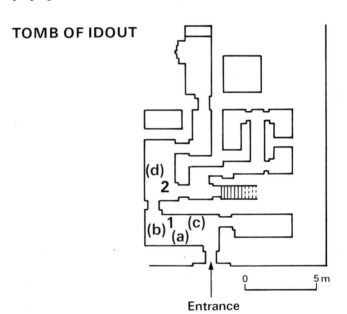

Entrance

TOMB OF PRINCESS IDOUT (daughter of Unas)

This tomb, situated near the southern wall of the Step Pyramid of Zoser, was excavated in 1927 and proved to have been usurped in the 6th Dynasty. It contains ten chambers, five of which are storerooms. Two of the remainder are noteworthy for the variety of nautical sports, sea and river scenes. Princess Idout was undoubtedly fond of the great outdoors.

In chamber (1), at (a) is a scene of fishing with trap nets. The left-hand wall (b) shows peasants being brought to justice. Note the equipment of the scribes. On the rear wall (c) are more fishing scenes. Note the four-pronged spear.

A farmer carries a calf across a canal. (Tomb of Kagemni)

In the second chamber (2) there is a well-preserved scene on the left-hand wall (d). Note the hippo fighting (in the bottom row), and one hippo is giving birth, its offspring destined to fall into the waiting jaws of a crocodile. Cattle are encouraged to cross a canal by following a calf held on the back of a peasant. Towards the centre of the wall is a large tree. Note the mongoose, the fox with a bird in its mouth, and the bird sitting on eggs in her nest.

The other chambers of this tomb contain scenes of offerings, and of sacrifice of bulls.

THE TOMB OF NEBET

Nebet was the wife of Unas. Her tomb was one of three discovered by the Egyptian Department of Antiquities in 1944. It is a small tomb, which was never completed. On the left-hand wall of the first chamber the theme is drawn in red near the door, but further along the wall are delightful fishing scenes in painted relief, with a charming family of hoopoe birds in the bulrushes.

The pale-skinned Nebet dominates the rear wall. She wears a jewelled collar, bracelets and anklets, and her diadem is held in

150

position by means of a wide ribbon tied behind her head. She holds a lotus blossom to her nose.

The right-hand wall has further marsh scenes. The crocodile, lurking in the waters, is most realistically painted.

The inner chambers of the tomb, which contain the usual scenes of offerings and aspects of everyday life, are in poor condition.

TOMB OF IRUKA-PTAH (open by special permission)

This tomb was discovered in 1964 while excavations were being carried out on the causeway linking the mortuary temple of the pyramid of Unas to the valley temple. Iruka-Ptah was Overseer of the Royal Slaughterhouse, and his tomb retains its vivid colouring to this day. It contains ten full-length statues of the deceased, eight of which are sculptured side by side and plastered with stucco; the last three of the group depict a young man with a moustache.

On the opposite wall there are four relief representations, over which the deceased, seated before a table of offerings, presides: the slaughter of the animals, sectioning and skinning, while a scribe keeps record. The tomb has become known as the 'Butcher's Tomb'. The quality of relief and high colour date it to the end of the 6th Dynasty.

The slaughter of bulls. (Tomb of Mereruka)

CHAPTER 6 NEW KINGDOM AND LATE PERIOD

Memphis was the principal seat of government in the New Kingdom (Chapter 7). It was to be expected, therefore, that the Sakkara necropolis should have a New Kingdom burial ground. A series of tombs belonging to the period were, in fact, identified and documented by Lepsius in the middle of the 19th century but they had been partly pillaged (as evidenced by various decorated fragments in the hands of private collectors and in the museums of the world), and covered with sand.

In 1970, Geoffrey Martin and Hans Schneider, in a joint expedition sponsored by the Egypt Exploration Society of London and the National Museum of Antiquities in Leiden, embarked on the relocation of the already documented New Kingdom tombs. They were searching, in particular, for the tomb of an official called Maya who served in the reign of Tutenkhamon. In 1975 the Tomb of Haremhab was discovered.

TOMB OF HAREMHAB (not open to the public)
Haremhab was the army general who made his first appearance on the political scene in the reign of Akhenaten, who served also under Tutenkhamon and, after the short reign of Ay, became pharaoh of Egypt himself. Finding this tomb was, therefore, an unexpected and valuable reward; it was built when he was still a general, before excavation of his royal tomb in the Valley of the Kings was started.

One inscribed block of stone discovered in the tomb is of historical importance. It bears parts of the *cartouches* of Tutenkhamon which were usurped by Haremhab, thus settling any controversy of the date of the tomb.

Some of the reliefs are in good condition and retain their original colour. Haremhab is depicted at different periods of his life: there is a conventional representation of him as a young man, and another realistically carved as an ageing man. Other preserved scenes show Haremhab seated before a table of offerings, and a charming relief of three attendants holding felines, probably lions.

Museums around the world, especially the Museum of Leiden, which possess fragments or blocks from this tomb, have been approached and will send plaster casts to Egypt to enable as complete a restoration of the tomb as possible. Meanwhile construction of a protective plaster roof is being completed (See Work in Progress Nos. 9, 10, 11, pages 177 and 178)

THE APIS TOMBS (Serapeum)

General

When this vast sepulchre was discovered by the French archaeologist Mariette in 1851 it was found that the rock-hewn galleries date primarily to three periods: the earliest to the reign of Ramses II, which was extended by his son Khaemwas; a second gallery to the reign of Psammetek I in the 26th Dynasty; and the third, the main gallery, to Ptolemaic times. They are hewn out of solid rock, and the flanking chambers contain huge granite sarcophagi, of an average weight of 65 tonnes each, and measuring some 4 metres in length, 2 metres in width, and $3\frac{1}{2}$ metres high. Most of the lids are of solid granite; five are composed of separate pieces of stone cemented together.

In the words of Mariette:

'[when] I first penetrated into the sepulchre of the Apis, I was so overcome with astonishment that, though it is now five years ago, the feeling is still vivid in my mind. By some inexplicable accident one chamber of the Apis tombs, walled up in the thirtieth year of Ramses II, had escaped the general plunder of the monuments, and I was so fortunate as to find it untouched. Three thousand seven hundred years had had no effect in altering its primitive state. The finger mark of the Egyptian who set the last stone in the wall built up to cover the door, was still visible in the mortar. Bare feet had left their traces on the sand strewn in a corner of this chamber of the dead; nothing had been disturbed in this burying-place where an embalmed ox had been resting for nearly fourteen centuries.' (Ebers, G. Egypt, Cassell, Petter, Galpin & Co. p. 161)

When Mariette entered the galleries, he found that most of the sarcophagus lids had been pushed aside and the contents had been pillaged. One, however, had been left intact. Robbers had been unsuccessful in their efforts to open it and, in fact, Mariette had to use dynamite. Inside the sarcophagus he found a solid gold statue of a bull standing some 120 cm. high (Louvre), as well as alabaster vases and the inner sarcophagus. The mummy of the bull is now in the Agricultural Museum in Cairo.

APIS TOMBS

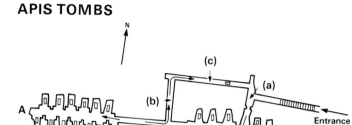

The mummified body of a young man with a gold mask was found in the Apis galleries with ornaments of gold and precious stones on his breast. Inscriptions indicate that this was the body of Ramses II's son Khaemwas, whom he appointed High Priest of Ptah, and who was said to have been a particularly pious man. In fact he inscribed on several of the pyramids at Sakkara and Abu Sir that he was desirous of restoring all important monuments of the ancient kings. It is strange that his body should have been buried among the mummies of the sacred bulls.

The discovery of the Apis tombs was of immense historical importance, for thousands of small votive tablets (mostly in the Louvre) yielded valuable information on the birth, death and date of burial of the Apis bulls. This has enabled Egyptologists to determine the exact duration of many of the pharaohs' reigns and their order of succession, especially during the Saite Period and in Graeco-Roman times.

The temple above the Apis tombs has entirely disappeared. An avenue of sphinxes led from this temple to a second temple, constructed by Nektanebos II, the last of the Egyptian rulers. This has also disappeared. However, after Alexander took possession of Egypt, the Ptolemaic rulers adorned a semi-circular space in front of Nektanebos' temple with statues of Greek philosophers, which can be seen in a depression, in a protective covering, almost immediately in front of the tented Rest House.

Description

A stone stairway descends to the entrance of the Serapeum, and we enter a corridor (a). The niches in the limestone walls held the votive tablets placed there by pilgrims to the site. Turning to the left we pass an enormous granite sarcophagus, inscribed with the name of the Persian King Artaxerxes, on our way to the main gallery (A)–(B). This gallery penetrates solid rock to a height of about 8 metres. Flanking it to left and right are chambers, also hewn out of the bedrock, containing the sarcophagi of the sacred bulls, each weighing between 60 and 80 tonnes. Twenty-four of the twenty-five were robbed in antiquity.

The lids of many of the sarcophagi are askew, giving the impression that they were gently thrust aside by the robbers. Yet some were so lodged into position that in recent times dynamite had to be used.

Some of the sarcophagi of the sacred bulls are highly polished and engraved with hieroglyphics. Some are decorated with the façade of a palace. Some are plain. Towards the end of the main gallery, to the right, one can descend to the chamber, and climb the wooden stairs to the top of the sarcophagus. Perhaps only by so doing do we realise the enormous size of these massive black and red granite coffers.

Retracing our steps from the end of the main gallery, we turn to the left (b), and then right (c). An empty sarcophagus almost blocks the route. And, a little further along, its lid may be seen. It appears that it was abandoned before the interment of the sacred bull, which would indicate that the cult was abruptly ended.

The Serapeum Way

Few visitors to Sakkara realise that the Apis tombs lay at the end of a processional avenue, known as the Serapeum Way, which, in Graeco-Roman times, extended from the cultivated land near the mortuary temple of Teti westwards to the Serapeum; the whole avenue was lined with sphinxes and chapels and as visitors made their way westwards to leave votive offerings at the Serapeum, they passed the statues of Greek philosophers shown in the photograph on p. 157.

The avenue has long been buried beneath garbage dumps and modern buildings, but in 1976/77 the Egypt Exploration Society, under the direction of Professor Harry S. Smith, conducted a survey, and subsequent excavation, of the mortuary temple of the pyramid of Teti. The aim was to examine Late Period temple precincts and catacombs where deified animals were interred. A burial ground for cats was discovered, and also one for the jackal, the animal associated with Anubis, the god concerned with mummification.

During excavations the team came across a mud-brick enclosure believed to be the embalmers' quarter of Memphis. (See the Embalming House of the Apis Bull pages 166 and 167)

LATE PERIOD
Saitic and Persian Tombs (*c.* 500 B.C.)

Three important tombs of the Persian period have been linked by means of passageways. They lie south of the Pyramid of Unas and belong to:

Psammetek (Chief Physician)
A spiral metal stairway leads 25 metres down the shaft, at the bottom of which is the burial chamber in which the limestone sarcophagus completely fills the area. Note the fine quality of the hieroglyphic inscriptions on the walls, which were copied from the Pyramid Texts.

Zannehibu (Commander of the King's Ships)
When opened, this tomb contained the mummy of the deceased, complete with gold mask, jewellery and precious amulets (Cairo Museum). The inscriptions on the walls of the tomb recount the career of the deceased.

Paydees
The tomb chamber has an arched ceiling which is painted in blue and decorated with stars of many colours. The walls are decorated with representations of offerings, which are in good condition. They are skilfully carved.

Saitic and Persian Shafts
In order to place sarcophagi at the bottom of the shafts, the Persians excavated two shafts, one narrower than the other, with a connecting horizontal passage at the bottom. The larger shaft would then be filled with sand on the top of which the sarcophagus was placed. When the sand was removed to the smaller shaft through the connecting passage, the sarcophagus subsided into position.

MONASTERY OF ST JEREMIAH
(5th Century Coptic Saint)

These ruins are situated at the edge of the desert to the left of the causeway leading to the Step Pyramid and some 500 metres distant.

They were discovered in 1905, and found to include two churches, cells and outbuildings as well as bakery, press-house, store-rooms etc. Some studies on the ruins showed that certain parts dated to the 4th Century, others to a later date, and several chambers appeared to have been renovated in the 9th Century. Parts of many New Kingdom monuments were found re-used in its buildings.

The main church was the latest construction site, and was formed like a basilica with a nave, two narrow aisles and three entrances. Most of the columns were in limestone, but four were in granite and three in marble.

All the stelae, paintings and fragments of mosaics were taken to the Coptic Museum in Cairo in 1909, and the site drew no more interest until 1980 when the German Archaeological Institute, under Dr. Peter Grossman, took out a short concession to excavate and restore some of the buildings, including a basilica.

The team included archaeologists and architects and the initial purpose of the project was to establish a detailed plan of the monastery, which covers about four acres; also to trace architectural developments during the 6th and 7th Centuries. Early brick structures were later faced with stone, and the monks reused the crypts and tombs of a Roman cemetery for their private use. They also built two churches (one of which has an unusual square ground plan) and two large halls for communal use to the north of the site.

In the 6th Century, monks were exempted from taxation, and this prompted a surge of monasticism, which had, until then, remained secret. Extensive building operations were carried out, of which this monastery is a fine example. In fact, built as it is on a spur at the edge of the desert, the Monastery of St. Jeremiah could be regarded as a Christian 'statement' rather than a place for withdrawal and spirituality. The absence of an enclosure wall is significant; monks were a prominent feature of the Sakkara plateau until the 9th Century when the monastery was abandoned.

Statues of Greek philosophers once stood in front of the temple of Nectanebos.

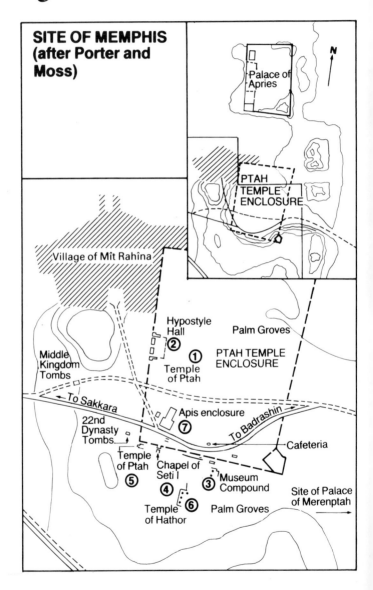

SITE OF MEMPHIS
(after Porter and Moss)

N

Palace of Apries

PTAH
TEMPLE
ENCLOSURE

Village of Mît Rahîna

Hypostyle
Hall
②

①
Temple
of Ptah

PTAH TEMPLE
ENCLOSURE

Palm Groves

Middle
Kingdom
Tombs

To Sakkara

Apis enclosure
⑦

To Badrashin

Cafeteria

22nd
Dynasty
Tombs

Temple
of Ptah
⑤

Chapel of
Seti I

④

③ Museum
Compound

Temple
of Hathor

⑥ Palm Groves

Site of Palace
of Merenptah

CHAPTER 7   MEMPHIS

General

Memphis was capital of Egypt for about a thousand years, and an important religious and commercial centre throughout the three thousand years of the country's ancient history. It was said to be founded by the first pharaoh (*c.* 3100 B.C.), it was honoured by its most famous kings, and it was the place where they were traditionally crowned. Memphis was a city lauded by the classical writers in glowing terms, visited by merchants, traders and sightseers, sought as a place of pilgrimage, or a place of refuge. It was the site where Alexander the Great was buried (before Ptolemy I moved his body to Alexandria), and where Amr Ibn al As signed his peace treaty with the Egyptians in 642 A.D. This was a city so great that any who sought control of Egypt knew that they had first to make themselves masters of Memphis.

The once rambling, heavily populated city owed its importance to its strategic position. King Narmer chose well when he set up his fortification, the 'White Wall' at the apex of the Delta, between the Two Lands of Upper and Lower Egypt. It was a suitable position for local trade as well as foreign commerce. Nubians and western Asiatics came to Memphis from earliest times; the regular flow of foreigners became a virtual influx in the Late Period, especially following the Persian occupation of Egypt. Coins and sculptures found in the ruins of Memphis show that Carians, Lydians, Attic Greeks and Macedonians came in great numbers as well as Semites, Syrians and Persians. Memphis was for them, in the words of the French scholar Gaston Maspero, '. . . what Cairo has long been for us moderns, the oriental city *par excellence*, the representation, the living symbol of Egypt.'

The analogy is apt: *Hikaptah*, 'House of the *ka* of Ptah', one of the names of Memphis, gave Egypt its name – it became *Aigyptos* in Greek and hence 'Egypt' – just as, today, the Arabic word for Egypt (Misr) is also the word for Cairo.

But Memphis is no more. It has suffered the ravages of war, fanaticism and time. Its monuments have been torn down, usurped, pillaged and used as quarry. Whatever remained has long been buried beneath alluvial soil that started to build up in medieval times; the Mameluks (originally slaves trained for service in the Sultan's bodyguard) neglected waterways, canals and dykes during their rule of Egypt. Each year the Nile flood poured over the land and found its level in the ruins of ancient monuments.

Layer upon layer of mineral-rich soil, between layer upon layer of habitation, led to the remaining ruins of the ancient city being almost totally submerged. Where once stood a mighty metropolis bustling with activity, described by Diodorus as having a circuit of 150 'stadia' (about eight miles long and four miles wide), there is today a scene of rural tranquillity. Villagers cultivate date-palm groves and grow crops in the enriched earth.

What we know of Memphis is drawn largely from the descriptions of classical writers who came to Egypt between the 5th Century B.C. and the early Christian era – Herodotus, Plutarch, Diodorus and Strabo – and from the funerary monuments on the necropolis of Sakkara. In addition, a wealth of information can be gleaned from inscribed blocks of stone that were re-used in later monuments, and inscriptions on statuary and objects taken from the site, which now adorn the museums of the world.

A statue of Ramses II behind the Museum Complex at Memphis.

Seated statue of Ptah, God of Memphis, flanked by goddesses holding children. *(Memphis)*

The central feature of the city of Memphis was the Temple of Ptah, one of the great gods of Egypt, whose national shrine was enlarged and embellished for thousands of years by successive pharaohs. Ptah was a patron deity of artists and craftsmen, and also a god associated with the creation of world order. A text that has survived in a late copy on what is known as the Shabako Stone (after the 25th Dynasty pharaoh who found it and ordered it to be re-copied), describes Ptah as 'He Who Created The All And Brought Forth The Gods. ...' The text continues:

'... He ... made the towns, founded the provinces, and placed the gods at their places of worship. He ... determined their offerings and founded their sanctuaries, and ... made their body as they desired. ...'

According to this text, Ptah's creative ability came about '... from what the heart had thought and the tongue had commanded ...'; in other words, through the spoken word.

The great **Temple of Ptah** within its huge **Enclosure** (1) must once have been a worthy rival to the Temple of Amon-Ra at Karnak; one of the reasons why so little of the Ptah Temple Complex survived, while that of Karnak has been well preserved is, quite simply, because Memphis lay in a limestone area and most of its monuments were built of this medium. When, in Roman times, cement was introduced as a building material, the monuments were destroyed and burned for lime content.

All that survives of the Great Temple of Ptah are the ruins of the **Hypostyle Hall** (2), which date to the reign of Ramses II. Measurements and studies of these show that Herodotus was not exaggerating when he described them as being made of stones '... which exceed(ed) in size those of any other temple in Egypt ... vast and well worthy of mention.' The Hypostyle Hall at Memphis was, in fact, larger than that of Karnak. Moreover, in place of a central row of columns, there were three rows, forming a double, rather than a single entrance. The columns were fashioned of red granite, the lower reaches of the entrance walls were lined with black basalt, the central gate and some of the engaged columns were of quartzite, and Egyptian alabaster door-jambs have been found. The multi-coloured effect must have been magnificent, especially since the flag-staffs would have been tipped with gold and the reliefs painted in bright colours.

An inscription near the second Cataract gives an idea of the magnificence of the Great Temple of Ptah. Ramses II – who ordered the construction of the enclosure wall (of which little remains) and carried out extensive building projects, including no less than four

Four alabaster altars.

separate temples within it – is depicted in conversation with the god Ptah of Memphis. The king says:

'*I have enlarged thy house in Memphis, protected with everlasting works, with excellent labor, in stone, wrought with gold and genuine costly stones, I constructed thy forecourt on the north with an august double facade before thee. Their doors are like the horizon of heaven, causing (even) strangers to praise thee...*' (Breasted, J. *Ancient Records of Egypt*, Vol. III p. 181.)*

No evidence of this northern gateway remains. But in the time of Herodotus the eastern gateway did. He claimed it to be the most splendid: '... for all the porticos have sculptured figures and an infinite variety of architecture, but this most of all.' This too, has disappeared. All that survives on site is the crumpled western gate built by Ramses II and part of the processional causeway leading from the south towards the position of the Museum Compound.

The Museum Compound (3), situated beside the main road, contains statues, stelae and miscellaneous objects collected from the environs of Memphis. The most important are:

The Alabaster Sphinx: This is the largest statue ever found fashioned of this stone. It weighs some eighty tons, and although somewhat weathered, is still impressive. It is an early 18th Dynasty statue, attributed to either Amenhotep I or Thutmose I.

The Stela of Apries, which was erected by this 26th Dynasty pharaoh; it bears figures of Ptah and of Sokar, the god that gave Sakkara its name. It is a huge, round-topped stela made of whitish-grey Nubian sandstone, and it is over three metres high and 77 centimetres thick. It is one of the most historically important monuments in Memphis, bearing a public announcement (badly eroded) dedicating certain lands to the god Ptah of Memphis. The text seems to be a renewal of an older decree ('in order to perpetuate what has been done by the Ancestors'). It reads:

'*The King's self (says): My Majesty has decreed that the District near Memphis, in the midst of the Great Canals (?), be dedicated for a God's revenue of my Father Ptah ... together with all its serfs, all (its) large and small cattle, and every(thing) that comes out of it, in (country) or town, as well as the farm-land of the gods and goddesses which is there. ... My Majesty has further decreed that all marsh-land and all arable land that are adjacent to this District be dedicated to my father Ptah ... that this region be reserved and protected, for my Father Ptah. ...*' At the end of the long text the date is given: '... Regnal-year 13, Month 4 of Akhet ...' (translation by B. Gunn). In other words, the stela dates to about 576 B.C.

*Published by Russell and Russell Publications, New York.

The **Colossus of Ramses II** is the main feature of the Museum Compound. It is of hard, fine-quality limestone and lies in a special shelter. Part of the crown and the lower legs are missing, but the sturdy torso, details of the muscles of the legs and arms, as well as the pharaoh's handsome features, show the high standard of craftsmanship in the New Kingdom. The royal cartouche bearing the king's name is carved on the right shoulder, on the chest and on his girdle.

Ramses II, who built extensively at Memphis even after he founded his new capital in the north-eastern Delta, erected his huge statues in pairs. It would not be unreasonable to suppose, therefore, that this limestone statue, the red granite monolith from Memphis which today adorns Station Square in Cairo, as well as the fragments of statues in other qualities of granite, all had counterparts adorning entrances to the various monuments of Memphis.

The **Chapel of Seti I** (4), was discovered by chance in 1947 when the Department of Antiquities decided to dig a trench around the Great Temple of Ptah, in an effort to drain subsoil water and facilitate excavation and reconstruction. It contains three seated statues, which are unique. They are of the god Ptah seated between two unidentified goddesses both nursing Seti I as a child. The young king is seated on their laps facing Ptah (photo on p. 161). *The chapel may only be seen with special permission.*

The **Small Temple of Ptah** (5), which lies well below the level of the cultivated land west of the chapel of Seti I, was partly excavated by the University Museum team of the University of Pennsylvania in 1955; excavations were halted due to the level of the sub-soil water. It is a regular New Kingdom Temple comprising entrance pylon, open court, hypostyle hall and sanctuary. The sanctuary comprises three chambers, dedicated to the triad of Memphis: Ptah, his consort Sekhmet and their son Nefertum. Ptah has the central chamber which is approached by a few steps, representing the primeval hill.

It is interesting to observe that during the prosperous 18th and 19th Dynasties, many Old and Middle Kingdom monuments were stripped of blocks of stone, which were subsequently reused: a Middle Kingdom inscription from the Great Temple of Ptah, for instance, was reused by Ramses II for the base of a statue, and the **Small Temple of Ptah** (5) contains at least one reused block of Amenhotep III.

Even more interesting is the fact that the monuments of the pharaohs who did this, suffered the same fate: When the **Tombs of**

the High Priests of the 22nd Dynasty (situated west of the small Temple of Ptah) were discovered, the outer and inner lintels of a doorway were found to have been constructed of usurped stone. The outer lintel showed a pharaoh – at first thought to be Haremhab but later identified as Tutenkhamon – kneeling before the gods Sokar and Hathor. The scene on the inner lintel was of Seti I depicted running towards a seated goddess. Both objects are in Cairo Museum.

Also in Cairo Museum is the ceiling of the burial chamber of Prince Sheshong, which was originally a stele of Amenhotep III. Moreover, the Prince was buried in a sarcophagus of a man called Amenhotep Hwi, a vizier under Ramses II. This sarcophagus is now in the Museum Compound at Memphis.

The **Palace of Merenptah** was discovered by a team from the University of Pennsylvania when clearing a mound lying south-east of the Great Temple of Ptah. The palace seems to have been burned soon after the pharaoh's death, but fortunately enough material survived to enable the reconstruction of what is considered the most well preserved throne room to have survived of a pharaoh of the New Kingdom; the columns were encrusted with faïence.

The beauty of this monument is especially remarkable when we remember that this was not a palace in the capital (which was then Per Ramses in the Delta), but a provincial city. (The throne room has been transported to the Museum of Philadelphia.)

The **Temple of Hathor** (6) was a chance discovery made in 1967 when soldiers were digging a bunker at the military camp located in the area. A temple to this goddess was known to exist in Memphis from frequent textual references but its position was not known.

The Temple of Hathor is a New Kingdom monument, built by Ramses II. Only the central part has been cleared, to a depth of half the height of the "Hathor-columns'.

The **Embalming House of the Apis Bull** (7) was discovered in 1941 by the Egyptian Antiquities Service. It was at first identified as the place described by the classical writers as the Stall of the Living Apis. Among the objects found were huge beds made of alabaster and decorated along the sides with the elongated bodies of lions in relief, as well as four alabaster altars.

The Apis bull, as already mentioned, was sacred to Memphis, and Herodotus described a court where it was kept and fed. He wrote: '... *this court has an inner colonnade all round it and many carved figures; the roof is held up by great statues twelve cubits high for pillars.*' Plutarch wrote of a hall for the bull adjoining the Temple of Ptah:

'... There were two compartments ... and in the front a magnificent peristyle court.... His food was selected with the greatest care, and lest in his state of confinement he should grow too fat, he was not given the water of the Nile to drink.'

When Strabo came to Egypt some five centuries after Herodotus he described:

'... a kind of sanctuary. In front ... is situated a court in which there is another sanctuary belonging to the bull's mother. Into this court they set Apis loose at a certain hour, particularly that he may be shown to foreigners; for although people can see him through the window in the sanctuary, they wish to see him outside also, and when he has finished a short bout of skipping in the court, they take him back again ...'

The alabaster beds are undated. Inscriptions on the monuments make mention of Seshonk I, Necko II and Amasis of the 26th Dynasty. (See Work in Progress, Chapter 8).

The above summarises the rather meagre remains of the ancient city of Memphis. Of the assemblage of buildings, their size, number

A drain and basin at the end of the sloping alabaster table. (Memphis)

and where the different internal communities were located, we know nothing. We do know that Egypt's greatest kings honoured the site. Amenemhet III, who established the capital in the Fayoum area in the Middle Kingdom, built (if we are to believe Herodotus), a portal '... facing the north wind'; Ahmose, founder of the New Kingdom, reopened the limestone quarries at Tura, opposite Memphis, in order '... to cut out thence the best white stone of the hill country for the houses of the gods ... for the house of the divine Ptah of Memphis', as recorded in a rock inscription; there is evidence that Amenhotep IV (who later changed his name to Akhenaten) built a temple at Memphis for the worship of The Aten, and Tutenkhamon wrote his famous Restoration Decree while residing '... in his palace, which is in the estate of Akheperkare ...' (identified from the monuments of Seti I and Ramses II as Memphis).

Although the most favourable location for the royal residence, due to the prevailing winds, would be to the north of the city, the site undoubtedly shifted from period to period. The ruins of Merenptah's Palace, for example, were found south-east of the Great Temple of Ptah.

The Palace of Apries (Hophra of the Bible) is a huge elevation lying to the north of Memphis. It is a sort of platform – now much depleted – reinforced by mud-brick cells or divisions that were filled with debris, broken pottery, stone chips and domestic rubbish. This platform supported a huge palace, the size of which can be gauged from the segments of limestone columns and two palm capitals that lie scattered around the top. Its attribution to Apries rests on crude cartouches bearing the name of this 26th Dynasty pharaoh. In fact, it is of unknown date.

When Strabo visited Egypt about 27 B.C. he described the buildings of the palace '... in ruins and deserted ... situated on a height and extend(ing) down to the ground of the city below'. It is tempting to postulate that he was, in fact, referring to this monument of Apries, and that his description of lakes in front of Memphis referred to the Sacred Lake of the Temple of Ptah.

The palace must have once been a magnificent structure, commanding a view of the river Nile, with broad stretches of fertile land on each side, and the whole of the desert plateau to the west, dominated by the Step Pyramid of Zoser.

When in Memphis the king had his entourage of officials ranging from the 'General of the Residence' to the 'Royal Herald' and 'Overseer of Royal Ships', as well as servants for the various household activities, specialists for the royal toilet, and entertainers.

Extending southwards was the Memphite metropolis at the centre of which was the Temple of Ptah with its scribal school, and medical centre under a 'Head of Physicians'. Since the High Priest of Ptah usually bore the title 'Director of Craftsmen', perhaps the various industries for the manufacture of statuary, furniture, pottery, gold and metalwork, were situated nearby. Further afield, perhaps in the desert, were camps for the training of the militia under a 'Commander of the Army of the Lord of the Two Lands'.

It would be reasonable to infer that in times of uncertainty the population of the surrounding areas sought security within the fortified walls of Memphis, or at least drew towards the denser, more protected areas.

Memphis was undoubtedly Egypt's most conservative, and, at the same time, most cosmopolitan city. It combined a strong local identity based on deep-rooted traditions, with a remarkable absorptive capacity to tolerate other peoples' diverse beliefs and practices. This was due, in no small part, to the fact that Memphis was a river port and a commercial centre that saw the exchange of populations, goods and ideas from early times. Memphites were used to the sight of foreigners, and welcomed them.

In 568 B.C., under King Apries, Jewish exiles were received at Memphis. Forty years later, under King Amasis, Ionian and Carian refugees also settled down there. Although the different races mingled freely in a colourful spectacle around the river port and in the market places, each had a separate (as yet unidentified) quarter: the Phoenicians lived in the 'Tyrian Camp'. The Carians – Indo-Europeans who had settled in Greece – lived within the 'Carian Wall'. Syrians and other Semites occupied a section of the city where they built temples to their own gods, Baal, Astarte and Artastas.

The Egyptians had no objection to the immigrant communities honouring their own gods in their own temples within the city limits. In fact, temples to foreign deities were so familiar a sight at Memphis, that if a prayer to a local god proved to be ineffectual, Egyptians sometimes invoked Syrian gods.

Even after the Ptolemies inherited Egypt after the death of Alexander the Great, and made Alexandria the capital of Egypt, they continued to honour Memphis. Ptolemy I caused Alexander's body to be laid in state and preserved at Memphis; Ptolemy IV built a structure '. . . of red granite at the eastern entrance to the Temple to Ptah', and Ptolemy V is immortalised on his coronation on the famous Rosetta Stone in these words: '. . . a decree of the priests of

Ruins of Memphis. (1977)

Memphis conferring divine honours on Ptolemy V, Epiphanes, King of Egypt.'

The word 'Memphis' no longer exists in Egypt. The name is a Greek derivation of *Men-nefer*, the name of the pyramid of Pepi I. However, the villagers of Mit Rahina, who live on a mound that rises above the floodplain that once stood in the very heart of the ancient city, call their village *Menf* or *Manf*. Whether they adopted this name to please early archaeologists and travellers because they heard them talk about 'Men-nefer', or whether the built-up area gradually crept beyond the site of Pepi's pyramid in the direction of Mit Rahina and the tradition has, in fact, survived through the ages, is not known. Nor is it clear why the ancient capital should have come to bear, as its most enduring name, that of the pyramid and 'pyramid town' of a late Old Kingdom pharaoh.

CHAPTER 8   WORK IN PROGRESS

MEMPHIS
Despite its importance and continuous occupation for thousands of years, only a small part of the central city of ancient Memphis has ever been excavated. In fact, not more than ten per cent. The first comprehensive study of the site was made by Flinders Petrie working for Britain's Egypt Exploration Society in 1908–1913. This was followed by several excavations by the Egyptian Antiquities Service between 1940–1956, and the University of Pennsylvania worked at the site between 1954–1955. Since then excavations have been sporadic and short-lived. Yet the rich potential of the site is apparent from the many discoveries that have been made by chance.

The Temple of Hathor, as already mentioned, was discovered by modern soldiers when digging a bunker. The Chapel of Seti I was found when a drain was being dug around the Temple of Ptah – at which time scores of 26th Dynasty bronze statuettes of various deities were also found. A Middle Kingdom cemetery was discovered because it lay in the path of a road that was being constructed from Badrashin to Sakkara in 1954; the road was halted and further clearance of the site led to the discovery of a flanking Middle Kingdom settlement (leading to speculation as to whether the tombs were built within, or just outside, the town area of Memphis). And a resident of Badrashin decided to build a Cafeteria on his land and found fragments of so many varieties of stone that it can only be concluded that they came from numerous destroyed colossi.

1 **The Survey of Memphis** is an Egypt Exploration Society project under the directorship of David G. Jeffreys; the coming years will bear witness to the largest operation Memphis has ever known, not only in its size but in the vision of what it hopes to accomplish. The aim, at this stage, is to draw together all existing material: monuments that survive on site, those taken to Museums around the world (including those in London, Cambridge, Manchester, Paris, Brussels, the Hague, Chicago and Philadelphia, apart from the Cairo Museum of Antiquities), and from some as yet unpublished studies from earlier excavations.

Professor Harry S. Smith of University College London, who began an initial field survey in 1981–82 maintains that a great deal has already been done that is not known, and that a compendium of known material is necessary before opening up new sites. The long-term goal of the survey is ambitious; to draw up a stratified map of ancient Memphis giving, where possible, ground plans of different structures at various stages of history.

2 The Apis House Project

This is a project of the Institute of Fine Arts of New York University, under the auspices of the American Research Centre in Egypt. It started with a survey of the standing remains at the site in 1982, including those structures now visible to visitors, which had been subject to earlier clearance operations. The Field Directors, Michael and Angela Milward Jones point out that these belonged to several different phases of development; the later structure, of limestone, was extensively damaged in antiquity by stone robbers who were active after the temples had fallen out of use, and who were in search of stone suitable for burning for lime, or for building material. This later stone structure also contained blocks bearing hieroglyphic inscriptions which probably date to times earlier than the monument itself, since they have been reused, sometimes more than once.

Work so far carried out has demonstrated one of the major problems in interpreting the remains of monumental buildings in urban areas such as Memphis, where concentrated occupation over a long period meant that structures were forever being pulled down and rebuilt, using the same stones over and over again, and finally burning them for lime content for cement.

The Apis House project has now moved to the second stage: new excavations. Already, in 1984, remains of earlier mud-brick buildings had been found outside the main stone Apis House. These form the oldest remains of buildings yet identified at the site, and may be linked with the inscribed blocks bearing the names of the 21st Dynasty king Sheshong I, and the 26th Dynasty rulers Necho II and Amasis.

SAKKARA

The monuments to be seen on the plateau today represent a mere fraction of what still lies beneath the sand. Five years ago an experiment was carried out by the Standard Research Institute of California using portable acoustic sounding equipment and other modern devices. It was hoped that the results would lead to the integration of scientific methods into standard archaeological procedures. In other words, the aim was to identify potential tombs and monuments, and thus facilitate the work of Egyptologists in excavation and restoration.

A team of engineers and physicists with some geological and geophysical experience, worked alongside Egyptologists on the plateau. The results were inconclusive. The equipment yielded abundant evidence of irregularities in the strata, but provided no clue as to whether these were man-made or natural; only further excavation would show whether a tomb, tunnel, shaft or natural fissure had been identified. This, of course, defeated the original purpose of the experiment, which was to save time, money and effort.

The official report did, however, confirm that the Sakkara plateau is literally riddled with sand-filled depressions. Any one of these could be the top of a shaft leading to a tomb, and we can confidently look forward to continued discoveries in the coming years.

OLD KINGDOM MONUMENTS

3 **Tomb of Ka-Menekh** (High Priest and Administrator of the Palace). The chance discovery of this 5th Dynasty tomb in the Spring of 1983 was made by Said el Fikey, Director of Antiquities at Sakkara, while clearing the Causeway of Unas as part of the overall plan to facilitate the movement of tourists. Due east of the tombs of Niankh-Khnum and Khnum-Hotep, seven shafts were discovered. They proved to be destroyed and pillaged rock-tombs filled with debris; it was decided to fill the depression and continue work.

Wind-blown sand had accumulated south of the causeway (near the tomb of Nefer), which provided convenient fill. Removal of the sand led to the discovery of a multiple tomb with five shafts and four false doors, one belonging to Ka-Menekh, the owner of the tomb. It is in a fairly good state of preservation, some of the reliefs retaining their original colour. One representation shows Ka-Menekh with his son 'Ka-Menekh the Younger' beside him.

The shaft at the entrance to the tomb contained amulets, beads and the mummies of a boy and a man. The former, in a wooden box, is well-preserved and, like the mummy of Nefer, is one of the earliest ever found intact. The mummy of the boy is dressed with kilt and sash. Clearance of the tomb continues.

4 **Tomb of Isisi-Ankh** (Seal-bearer and Treasurer of the King). The discovery of this tomb in the winter of 1982 also occurred by chance. Part of a lintel was noticed to the north of the Zoser

Complex after a sandstorm. Further clearance revealed a tomb belonging to an important 5th/6th Dynasty official, whose many titles included 'overseer of boats'.

It is a large tomb, some fifteen metres long and twenty-five wide, comprising entrance hall with columns and five small chambers. Several objects were found inside the tomb including two texts written on papyrus, two sailing oars and some pottery.

The tomb walls show that the original stone was marked into registers in red paint, ready for wall decoration; when the quality of the stone was found to be inferior, the interior of the entire tomb was plastered and painted with scenes. This technique of painting on plaster, used in the noblemens' tombs on the Theban necropolis, is unique at Sakkara.

Restoration of the tomb is going ahead. Some of the fallen blocks have been cemented in their original positions, the delicate paintings have been treated and will be glassed for protection, and the tomb will be roofed over. Meanwhile the two oars and vessels are being restored and the papyri – inscribed on both sides in black ink – are being studied.

5 Tomb of Khewi and others

At the end of August 1983 a project was started by Macquarie University, Sydney, under the directorship of Naguib Kanawati in association with Egyptologists attached to the Egyptian Antiquities Organisation. The site, situated immediately to the north of the tombs of Mereruka and Kagemni, was first excavated by Zaki Saad some forty years ago, and subsequently recorded by the epigraphic survey of the Egypt Exploration Society.

Clearance is going ahead in leaps and bounds, and though Kanawati emphasises that the aim of the project is not necessarily to find objects 'but to understand more about some of the obscure transition periods of the Old Kingdom', some objects are coming to light. These include several Old Kingdom false doors in limestone, some Late Period bronzes, a gold earring, and several, as yet unexplained, dual burials; these are of a man and woman interred together, in one case with a child between them, and point to the possibility of the outbreak of an epidemic.

Kanawati feels sure that the stone mastaba of Khewi and others were *not* 6th Dynasty tombs as stated in the epigraphic survey (based, no doubt, on their proximity to the 6th Dynasty Pyramid of Teti), but were, in fact, part of a 5th Dynasty cemetery that extended north-east from the pyramid of Userkaf, towards the site presently being excavated. 'We shall continue to clear to the north and to the west of the mastabas of Mereruka', says Kanawati, 'and I am confident that what we will find beneath the sand, is a 5th Dynasty cemetery.'

6 Tombs of Nikau-Isesi and Ptah-Shepses-pu

These two 5th/6th Dynasty tombs lie north of the mastaba of Ankh-mahor. They are in fairly good condition, and restoration is being conducted by Mahmoud Abdel Razek. The tomb of Nikau-Isesi, who bore the title of Treasurer, shows the owner supervising the assessment of wheat and its storage in granaries, and also some hunting scenes in well-preserved colour.

7 The Pyramids of Merenre and Pepi I (6th Dynasty)

A mission of the French National Centre for Scientific Research (CNRS), in collaboration with the Egyptian Antiquities Organisation, continues work on these two 6th Dynasty pyramids in South Sakkara. Professor Jean Leclant is in charge of excavations, and reconstruction is under the supervision of Jean-Philippe Lauer.

Egyptologists excavating the Pyramid of Userkaf.

Great interest is being focused on the Pyramid Texts; first, because they reveal a later stage in the development of the language than those found in earlier pyramids; secondly because the texts contain utterances, not common in other pyramids, which will hopefully cast light on the religious beliefs of the Old Kingdom.

Clearance and restoration of the tomb chambers of the Pyramid of Merenre have proven to be extremely demanding. This was not only because the pyramid was built of poor quality stone (apart from the outer facing) but also because it was plundered in antiquity. During the clearance operations sustaining walls had to be constructed, and hundreds of fragments of the Pyramid Texts collected and documented. After careful drawings of these have been completed, they will be matched up and studied.

The texts inscribed in the corridor of the Pyramid of Pepi I are exceptionally beautiful. They are smaller in size than those in the burial chamber, are filled with green pigment and painstakingly carved. Even miniature pots are worked in exquisite detail, and the tiniest birds have minute details of wings and feathers.

When the area around the Pyramid was being cleared, the team unexpectedly came across the Mortuary Temple of the Pyramid of Pepi I, and it was decided to apply for an extension of the 10-year project, and run concurrently the study of the Pyramid Texts and the restoration of the Mortuary Temple which is a magnificent, spacious and elegant complex. It includes huge courtyards, double-storied store-rooms, marble flagstones, and drains leading from ablution basins. There are also ruins of columns and huge sections of an unusual curved ceiling, decorated with stars.

NEW KINGDOM MONUMENTS

8 **The Tomb of Aper-el** dates to the 18th Dynasty. It is situated south of the Sakkara plateau, facing the east (beneath the Resthouse of the Antiquities Organisation). It was discovered by Alan Zivie working for the French Institute of Archaeology and is one of several rock-hewn tombs in the area. It is unique at Sakkara in having representations of the sun disks of the Aten, done in the revolutionary style of the 'Amarna Period' as well as the conventional reliefs.

9 **Tomb of Paser** (19th Dynasty)
Following the discovery of the Tomb of Haremhab (p. 151), Geoffrey Martin felt confident of finding more New Kingdom tomb chapels in the burial ground south of the Causeway of Unas. He was

not disappointed. Three tombs were discovered in 1981.

Paser was a royal scribe and the Overseer of Builders in the reign of Ramses II. His simple tomb, made of mud-brick, comprises a cult chapel with an antechamber in front of it flanked by vaulted storerooms. The tomb was never completed, but there is indication that the (missing) roof of the chapel supported a pyramidion of mud-brick.

10 **Tomb of Raia,** the Chief Singer of Ptah, is a simple, rectangular chapel of limestone, built on the south wall of Paser's tomb. Two columns were originally set, askew, at the entrance. Only the stumps remain. Some of the reliefs are in good condition and are extremely expressive; one shows the wife of this lector priest weeping and embracing his upright, wrapped mummy. Female mourners of his family are also shown, as well as a blind choir from the Temple of Ptah.

One beautiful and well-preserved scene is that of Raia, rendered as a blind harpist, before the seated figure of Ptah of Memphis and the goddess Hathor. Geoffrey Martin describes this as 'the best example of a Memphite New Kingdom tomb chapel *in situ*.'

11 **Tomb of Princess Tia,** the sister of Ramses II, daughter of Seti I, was discovered in the vicinity of the two tombs of the same period described above. Princess Tia married an official who also bore the name of Tia. Though not himself a member of the royal family, Tia was of some importance. He bore the titles of Treasurer and Overseer of the Temple of Ramses II in Memphis.

Much of this limestone tomb is well preserved. The unusual reliefs include a scene of Princess Tia and her husband adoring a procession of deities, and depicted carrying out the ritualistic journey to Abydos with horses on the barge with them. The fine quality of the reliefs is reminiscent of the Temple of Seti I at Abydos.

Work on this New Kingdom burial ground continues.

12 **Saitic and Persian monuments** (near entrance to the Pyramid of Userkaf). Aly el Kholy originally started a project to clear the entrance to this pyramid in 1976, and since then he has made a series of remarkable discoveries. The most recent was made in December 1982, when three papyri dating to the Saitic (26th Dynasty) period came to light in shafts south-east of the entrance to the pyramid. El Kholy has already cleared the two shafts, one wide

and the other smaller – typical of Saitic and Persian tombs (described on p. 155).

13 **Tomb of Beken-renef** (Bokkaris). Excavation and restoration of this funerary complex are part of a project by the Italian Institute of Archaeology of the University of Pisa, in collaboration with the Egyptian Antiquities Organisation. It is another Saitic period monument belonging to a Vizier and the project will continue in the coming season under the supervision of Professor Ida Bresciani.

14 **The Tomb of a woman of the Ptolemaic Period** was discovered in October 1982 as part of the plan to clear and landscape the necropolis for the enjoyment of tourists. While clearing near the famous mastaba of Ptah-Hotep, nine water wells that had been dug in the Old Kingdom, and later used as tombs, were found.

Only one of the five shafts has so far been cleared. In it were found the well-embalmed mummy of a woman, a funerary box painted with a falcon, a wooden statue of the lady herself, and jars containing ointments and offerings. One vessel was found to contain a piece of cheese. It was sent to Dr. Shawki Nakhla of the Department of Scientific Analysis of the Antiquities Organisation, and experiments revealed the existence of live bacteria; it had remained active for over twenty centuries!

Future Plans for Sakkara and Memphis
The Chairman of the Antiquities Organisation, Dr. Ahmed Kadry, has announced plans for a new museum to be built at Mit Rahina (Memphis). It has also been learned that a 'restoration centre' will be opened at Sakkara, in collaboration with the Italian Cultural Centre in Cairo, where five graduates of the Faculty of Egyptology will be invited to study the latest restoration methods of Italy.

TABLE OF KINGS OF THE EARLY DYNASTIC PERIOD AND THE 'OLD KINGDOM' (1st–6th Dynasties)

(All the pharaohs of the 1st and 2nd dynasties had two funerary monuments—one at Abydos and one at Sakkara.)

1st DYNASTY (3100–2890 B.C.)*

Narmer/Hor Aha (Menes)	Tradition accredits this pharaoh with uniting the Two Lands of Upper and Lower Egypt, founding Memphis and constructing the Temple of Ptah, the local deity.
Djer (Athothis)	Attempted to consolidate unity. According to Manetho this was the physician (not Imhotep), whose books on anatomy survived to Graeco-Roman times.
Meryet-Neith	Northern princess who was either Djer's Queen or succeeded him to the throne. Like the pharaohs she had two funerary monuments.
Djet (Uadji)	Architectural and artistic advancement indicates political stability. Serious 7-year famine.
Den (Udimu?)	Most prosperous reign of the 1st Dynasty. 'Double Crown' and '*Ni-sw-bity*' title first appeared. Heb-Sed festival documented.
Enezib (Miebis)	Evidence of political instability once more.
Semerkhet (Semempses)	Manetho records a 'time of very great calamities'.

*The names, dates and even order in which the pharaohs of the first two dynasties ruled are uncertain and controversial. Cambridge Ancient History, second edition, has been used as the guideline in the present work.

Ka'a (Bieneches)	Architectural innovations in his tomb at Sakkara. Writing had by this time developed considerably.

2nd DYNASTY (2890–2686 B.C)

Hotep-Sekhemui (Boethos)	Name means 'Two powers are at peace'. Manetho claimed that during his reign a chasm opened at Bubastis and that many perished.
Ra-Neb (Kaiechos)	Name means 'Ra is (my) Lord'. Worship of Apis bull established at Memphis, and Minervis Bull at Heliopolis.
Nynetjer (Binothris)	Indications of civil war. Manetho claimed that women were allowed to hold regal office for the first time.

tombs never found

Weneg/Sekhemib (Tlas)	Politico-religious revolution.
Sened/Sendji (Sethenis)	The name of this pharaoh survives only in the tomb of one of his officials.
Per-Ibsen	Breakaway government in Upper Egypt. Abandoned traditional Horus title, and adopted a Set title.
Khasekhem (Sesochris)	Re-established unity, and adopted (exceptionally) a Horus-and-Set title.
Khasekhemui (Cheneres)	Unity consolidated. Laid strong foundations for centralised government. Married princess of Lower Egypt (probably Zoser's mother). Both his tomb and a temple found at Hierakonpolis.

3rd DYNASTY (2686–2613 B.C.)

Sanakhte (Nebka)	May have been the elder brother of Zoser, buried in one of the galleries of the Step Pyramid.
Zoser (Neter-Khet)	Funerary Complex at Sakkara built by Imhotep. Exploitation of mineral resources. Tribes of northern Nubia suppressed.

Sekhem-Khet	Zoser's successor (probably his son). His unfinished Step Pyramid at Sakkara opened in 1954. Alabaster sarcophagus found empty.
Khaba	Step Pyramid at Zawiet el-Aryan.
Nebkare (Neb-ku)	Unfinished pyramid at Zawiet el-Aryan.
Huni	Builder of first 'true pyramid' at Meidum. His daughter married Sneferu.

4th DYNASTY (2613–2494 B.C.)

Sneferu	Two pyramids at Dahshur, south of Sakkara. Genial pharaoh who laid firm foundation for centralised government of 'The Great Pyramid Age'.
Khufu (Cheops)	Builder of the 'Great Pyramid' at Giza. His so-called 'Solar-Boat', buried in a rock-hewn pit to the south of the pyramid, was discovered by Kamal Malakh. Period of great productivity, due to centralised administration.
Redjedef	Pyramid (unfinished), at Abu Roash, north-west of Giza. Eight-year reign.
Khafre (Chephren)	Builder of the 'Second Pyramid' at Giza. Magnificent craftsmanship in his reign, particularly in royal sculpture.
Baufre	Reigned little more than one year.
Menkaure (Mycerinus)	Builder of the third pyramid on the Giza plateau, which was not finished when he died.
Shepseskhaf	May have been Menkaure's son, who had a short four-year reign. Built 'Mastaba el Fara'un', south of Sakkara, with bevelled roof (imitated at Giza in the 'unfinished fourth pyramid').
Dedefptah	Obscure and controversial period.

5th DYNASTY (2494–2345 B.C.)

Userkaf	His pyramid, near that of Zoser, was used as a quarry for a 26th Dynasty cemetery.

Sahure	First of the three 'divine' pharaohs. He set the precedent for constructing Sun Temples in addition to pyramids, at a new burial ground at Abu Sir.
Neferirkare	Died before completing his pyramid.
Shepseskare	Name known only from the 'Sakkara List'. No known monuments.
Neferefre	Unfinished pyramid. Little known about him.
Nyuserre	The Sun Temple of Nyuserre at Abu Ghurab contains well-preserved reliefs including records of names and careers of his various officials.
Menkauhor	Chief record of his reign is a rock inscription in Sinai. The names of his Sun Temple and Pyramid are known from records, but have not been discovered.
Djedkare (Isesi)	His pyramid is known as 'Haram el Shawwaf'. The Maxims of Ptah-hotep date to his reign. Several important persons connected with his reign built tombs along northern side of enclosure wall of Zoser's Step Pyramid (Vizier Shepsesre, two princesses—Isesiankh and Kaemtjenent—and Queen Meresankh, probably their mother).
Unas	Builder of first pyramid to be inscribed with Pyramid Texts. His name is carved on a boulder at Elephantine. Famine in his reign.

6th DYNASTY (2345–2181 B.C)

Teti (Othoes)	Manetho records that he was murdered by his own bodyguard. His two wives, Khuit and Iput, also buried at Sakkara.
Userkare	Little known of this pharaoh.
Meryre (Pepi I) (Piops)	Abundance of later literature refers to this pharaoh, who founded and restored many temples in various parts of the country. Memphis was named after his pyramid. Extensive mining and trading activities in his reign.

Merenre Son of Pepi I, who had a short reign.

Neferkare (Pepi II) 94-year reign. Impoverishment of the royal house.

Merenre II Of little significance.

Menkure Of little significance.

Under this Memphite Dynasty, the power of the pharaohs was limited and the governorates agitated for independence. Towards the end of the dynasty civil war broke out and the monarchy collapsed. The Old Kingdom came to an end.

(*See page 21 for subsequent Periods*)

Recommended for Further Reading

ADAMS, WILLIAM Y. *Nubia, Corridor to Africa,* Allen Lane, London, 1977

BREASTED, JAMES, *A History of Egypt,* Hodder & Stoughton, London, 1950

CLAYTON, PETER A. *The Rediscovery of Ancient Egypt: Artists and Travellers in the 19th Century,* Thames and Hudson, London 1982

FRANKFORT, H. *Ancient Egyptian Religion; an interpretation,* Harper, New York, 1961

GARDINER, SIR ALAN, *Egypt of the Pharaohs,* Oxford University Press, 1961

HABACHI, LABIB, *The Obelisks of Egypt,* Charles Scribner's Sons, New York, and J. M. Dent, London, 1978

KAMIL, JILL, *Luxor; a Guide to Ancient Thebes,* Longman, London and New York, 3rd ed. 1982
Upper Egypt; Historical Outline and Descriptive Guide to the Ancient Sites, Longman, London and New York, 1983
The Ancient Egyptians: A popular Introduction to Life in the Pyramid Age, American University in Cairo Press, 1984

KEES, H. *Ancient Egypt; a Cultural Topography,* Faber and Faber, London, 1961

KEATING, R. *Nubian Rescue,* Robert Hale, London and Hawthorn Books, New York, 1975

LEWIS, N. *Life in Egypt under Roman Rule,* Clarendon Press, Oxford, 1983

LICHTHEIM, MIRIAM *Ancient Egyptian Literature, A Book of Readings* (3 vols.), University of California Press, Berkeley, Los Angeles, London 1976

MEINARDUS, OTTO, *Christian Egypt; Ancient and Modern,* American University in Cairo Press, Cairo 1978

MURNANE, WILLIAM J. *The Penguin Guide to Ancient Egypt*, Penguin Books, Harmondsworth, 1983.

NIMS, CHARLES F. *Thebes of the Pharaohs,* Elek Books, London, 1965

SMITH, H. S. *A Visit to Ancient Egypt: Life at Memphis and Saqqara (c. 500–30 B.C.),* Aris and Phillips, Warminster, 1974

TRIGGER, BRUCE G. *Nubia under the Pharaohs,* Thames and Hudson, London, 1976

TRIGGER, B. G., KEMP, B. J., O'CONNER, D., LLOYD, A. B. *Ancient Egypt, A Social History,* Cambridge University Press, 1983

WEEKS, KENT, *et al., Egyptology and the Social Sciences,* American University in Cairo Press, Cairo 1979

WILSON, JOHN A. *The Culture of Egypt,* University of Chicago Press, 1956

INDEX

Page numbers in italics refer to illustrations.
References to maps, plans and diagrams are so described.

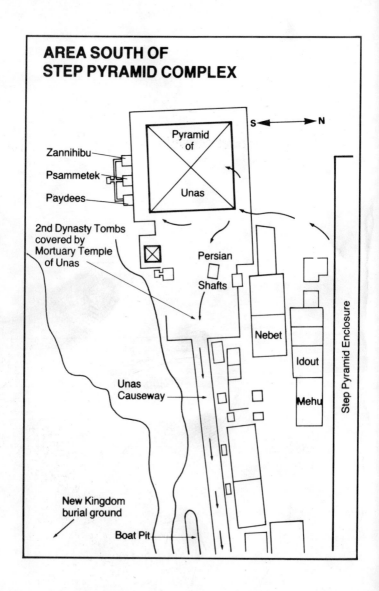

AREA SOUTH OF STEP PYRAMID COMPLEX

S ← → N

Zannihibu

Psammetek

Paydees

Pyramid of Unas

2nd Dynasty Tombs covered by Mortuary Temple of Unas

Persian

Shafts

Nebet

Idout

Mehu

Step Pyramid Enclosure

Unas Causeway

New Kingdom burial ground

Boat Pit